D1006535

Laughing

817.008
Lau

1219 80
8.95

Laughing

compiled by

Charles Keller

A Historical Selection of American Humor

Prentice-Hall, Inc.
Englewood Cliffs, N.J.

SANTA FE HIGH SCHOOL
LIBRARY

Copyright © 1977 by Charles Keller

All rights reserved. No part of this book may be reproduced in any form or by any means, except for the inclusion of brief quotations in a review, without permission in writing from the publisher.

Printed in the United States of America

Prentice-Hall International, Inc., London
Prentice-Hall of Australia, Pty. Ltd., North Sydney
Prentice-Hall of Canada, Ltd., Toronto
Prentice-Hall of India Private Ltd., New Delhi
Prentice-Hall of Japan, Inc., Tokyo
Prentice-Hall of Southeast Asia Pte. Ltd., Singapore

10 9 8 7 6 5 4 3 2

Library of Congress Cataloging in Publication Data

Main entry under title:

Laughing.

    Bibliography: p.
    Includes index.
    SUMMARY: A collection of American humor from colonial times to 1969 with introductions to the selections tracing the development of humor in the United States.
    1. American wit and humor. 2. Wit and humor, Juvenile. [1. Wit and humor] I. Keller, Charles.
PN6162.L28   817'.008   76-46321
ISBN 0-13-525790-5

Acknowledgements

The editor and publisher are grateful to the authors, agents, cartoonists, and publishers listed below for permission to reprint selections in this volume.

"The Ransom of Red Chief" from Whiriligigs by O. Henry, copyright 1907 by Doubleday and Co. Reprinted by permission of Doubleday and Co., Inc.

"Alibi Ike" from How to Write Short Stories by Ring Lardner, Copyright 1925. Copyright 1915 by Curtis Publishing Co. Renewal copyright 1943 by Ellis A. Lardner. Reprinted by permission of Charles Scribner's Sons.

"Why a Duck?" with the Marx Brothers from the film The Cocoanuts, copyright 1929. Reprinted by permission of Universal Pictures.

"Another Uncle Edith Christmas Story" from The Benchley Roundup edited by Nathaniel Benchley, copyright 1930 by Robert Benchley. Reprinted by permission of Harper and Row, Publishers, Inc.

"The Night the Bed Fell" from My Life and Hard Times by James Thurber, copyright 1933, 1961 by James Thurber and published by Harper and Row. Originally printed in The New Yorker. Reprinted by permission of Helen Thurber and Hamish Hamilton, London.

"Father Opens My Mail" from The Best of Clarence Day by Clarence Day, copyright 1948, renewed by Katherine Day, 1962. Reprinted by permission of Random House, Inc., Alfred A. Knopf.

"Pencil-Chewing" from A Pearl in Every Oyster by Frank Sullivan, copyright 1935. Renewed 1966. Reprinted by permission of Little, Brown and Co.

"Who's on First?" by Abbott and Costello from Who's on First?, edited by Richard J. Anabile, copyright 1972. Reprinted by permission of Darien House, Inc. Distributed by Avon Books.

"Fibber McGee and Molly" from the radio program Fibber McGee and Molly. Reprinted by permission of the National Broadcasting Corp.

"The Wonderful Adventures of Paul Bunyan" from The Wonderful Adventures of Paul Bunyan by Louis Untermeyer, copyright 1945, 1973 by George Macy, Companies Inc., New York. Reprinted by permission of The Heritage Club.

"Charles" from The Lottery by Shirley Jackson, copyright 1948. Reprinted by permission of Farrar, Straus and Giroux, Inc.

"She Shall Have Music" from The Many Loves of Dobie Gillis by Max Shulman, copyright 1951. Reprinted by permission of Harold Matson Co., Inc.

"Gracie Talks About Her Relatives" from the Burns and Allen television show. Reprinted by permission of Columbia Pictures Television.

"No Time For Sergeants" by Mac Hyman, copyright 1954. Reprinted by permission of Random House, Inc., Alfred A. Knopf.

"Chief White Halfoat" from Catch 22 by Joseph Heller, copyright 1955, 1961 by Joseph Heller. Reprinted by permission of Simon and Shuster.

"Dental or Mental, I Say It's Spinach" from The Most of S.J. Perelman by S.J. Perelman, copyright 1930, 1931, 1932, 1933, 1935, 1936, 1955, 1956, 1957, 1958. Reprinted by permission of Simon and Schuster.

"From the Back of the Bus" by Dick Gregory, copyright 1962 by Dick Gregory Enterprises, Inc. Reprinted by permission of E.P. Dutton and Co., Inc.

"Introducing Tobacco to Civilization" from the record album The Best of Bob Newhart. Reprinted by permission of Bob Newhart Publishing Co.

"Bunky" from The Neighbors Are Scaring My Wolf by Jack Douglas, copyright 1968 by Jack Douglas. Reprinted by permission of E.P. Dutton and Co., Inc.

Cartoons:

"Winnie Winkle" comic strip by Martin Branner, copyright 1927. Reprinted by permission of the Chicago Tribune-New York News Syndicate, Inc.

"Out Our Way" cartoon by J.R. Williams, copyright 1934. Reprinted by permission of Newspaper Enterprises Association. (NEA)

Cartoon from Up Front by Bill Mauldin, copyright 1944 by United Features Syndicate, Inc. Reprinted by permission of Bill Mauldin.

Cartoon by Paul Peter Porges, copyright 1957. Reprinted by permission of The American Legion Magazine and Paul Peter Porges.

Cartoon by John Gallagher, copyright 1967. Reprinted by permission of John Gallagher.

Books by Charles Keller

BALLPOINT BANANAS
TOO FUNNY FOR WORDS
LAUGH LINES
THE STAR-SPANGLED BANANA (with Richard Baker)
GOING BANANAS
PUNCH LINES
DAFFYNITIONS
GLORY, GLORY, HOW PECULIAR
THE LITTLE WITCH PRESENTS A MONSTER JOKE BOOK (with Linda Glovach)
GIGGLE PUSS

To my mother, Elizabeth

Contents

1. *Humor in the Colonies 1600–1780*   1

2. *Frontier Humor 1781–1860*   23

3. *A National Sense of Humor 1861–1919*   57

4. *Roaring with Laughter 1920–1929*   127

5. *Looking Back Laughing 1930–1939*   159

6. *American Humor Fights Back 1940–1949*   199

7. *America Laughs at Itself 1950–1959*   233

8. *American Humor Protests 1960–1969*   275

Bibliography   295

Index   297

Preface

A book like this with lots of funny stuff all sorted out and interpreted makes you wonder whether *laughing* really can be categorized and explained. A linguist once defined laughter as "a repetition of 'ah' with a glottal stop preceding each syllable." Ha, ha, ha—get it? It brings to mind one definition of an expert: someone who knows no more than you do, but who has it better organized and then explains it with slides.

We all know quite a bit about laughing from the viewpoint of participants, being members of the only species of intelligent laughers (hyenas don't count). Except for *nervous laughter* and its second cousin *hysteria*, we know that laughter feels good and that it follows from humor. We sense, moreover, that all humor is based on unlikely combinations of situations and words, these often tending to confuse simple and complicated things or to knock a high person down. For example, if a school principal posts a sign saying "The illumination is required to be extinguished when this area is not being utilized," and then a school kid writes below, "Turn off the juice when not in use," that's pretty funny, and it fills both our expectations.

It's an old joke, but a good one. When Bud Abbott tried to explain "Who's on first?" to Lou Costello, it was an elaboration of the same sort of thing.

All literary and professional humor derives in some way from the folk or traditional humor which has circulated by word of mouth before getting into print or on the airwaves. Therefore, a nation's laughing matters provide insight into that nation's values. Since we Americans have always had an irrepressible urge to laugh and to make others laugh, even sometimes at our own expense, the study of American humor is an important key to American character.

Charles Keller has arranged his selections chronologically, and in them he demonstrates how American humor mirrors characteristic features of our diverse population and history. Our humor specializes in the regional or ethnic stereotype; it features tricksters (particularly country hicks who, like Davy Crockett, one-up the city slicker); it delights in exaggerations delivered in dead-pan style; it is full of self-confident cockiness. American humor, in general, tends toward the short, the snappy, the outrageous; it blossoms forth as tall tales, bragging, hoaxes, spoofs, parodies, dialect dialogues, perverted proverbs, riddle jokes, daffy definitions, wisecracks, insults, and comebacks. Our jokes have few characters, one situation, and one punchline: *socko!* Finally, American humor is democratic; even presidents have been participants. Some were good oral humorists (like Abraham Lincoln and John F. Kennedy), some were the popular subject of humor (like Calvin Coolidge and Richard M. Nixon), and a few were both jokesters and the butts of jokes (like Harry S Truman and Lyndon B. Johnson).

Literary and other professional humorists adapt and adopt the forms and themes of folk humor; they also retain and make use of humor's social meaning. To echo the radio character, Molly; "It ain't funny, McGee!" Jokes can serve as fairly harmless outlets for strong feelings, are in no way meant to stir up antagonisms. Flip Wilson, Johnny Carson, Archie Bunker, and countless other humorists employ jokes that work in this way.

As Charles Keller points out in his introductions, American humor has changed as mass media have developed. Humor also changes with the times, with changing tastes, and it reflects war and peace, prosperity and recession, passing fads and popular fancies. Another typical American trait is to convert current events instantly into jokes—to laugh at life, insofar as it is possible. Some things about laughing, however, never seem to change. The way Artemus Ward spelled "snake"—s-n-a-i-k—is still worth a chuckle, although I cannot quite say why. And Gracie Allen's comeback at the end of every Burns and Allen radio and TV show was an American capsule comic classic, wrapping up mock innocence, quick wit, and deflating of the big shot in one tiny package:

George Burns: "Say 'Goodnight,' Gracie."

Gracie Allen: "Goodnight Gracie."

So—believe it or not—this book is not only fun, but it may help you understand American humor and your own favorite jokes a little better.

Jan Harold Brunvand
University of Utah

Laughing

1.

1600-1780

Humor in the Colonies

Verses for Every Month in the Year—Samuel Danforth

Epitaph Written 1728—Benjamin Franklin

The Flies—Benjamin Franklin

Epitaph On a Patient Killed by a Cancer Quack —Lemuel Hopkins

Yankee Doodle—A Patriotic Song

Joe Miller's Jokes

Introduction

Early American settlers chopped down forests and burned tree stumps to build their homes and sow their crops. They were accustomed to hardship, to the grueling labor of their daily lives. But they enjoyed being amused and having a good laugh as much as we do, and they provided it for themselves. They cracked a joke when fatigue hit them; they sang songs in front of home or tavern fire; and they told each other tall tales. True, their humor sprang from European sources, but there was a lack of sophistication about it that was different. It had a no-nonsense quality and a down-to-earth wit that poked fun at everything and everyone —rich and poor, snob and quack, loud-mouth and show-off. These early Americans even made fun of themselves.

At first, jokes and stories were passed from man to man, gaining richly in the retelling. But as time went on news-sheets were printed in large communities and those able to obtain them delighted in the comical tales and sayings they contained. Joke books such as Joe Miller's became popular, and Benjamin Franklin's almanac found its way into many hands. A new kind of humor was developing.

Colonial humor may not strike us as all that funny

today. But there was no malice. Unselfconscious silliness and jokes were at the expense of anyone who was boastful or pretentious, while plain speaking and a simple way of dressing were held in high regard. What we see revealed in the character of this kind of humor gives us a hint of what is to come.

Verses For Every Month in the Year
Samuel Danforth

[MARCH]

A Coal-white Bird appeares this spring
   That neither cares to sigh or sing.
This when the merry Birds espy,
   They take her for some enemy.
Why so, when as she humbly stands
   Only to shake you by your hands?

[APRIL]

That which hath neither tongue nor wings
   This month how merrily it sings:
To see such, out for dead who lay
   To cast their winding sheets away?
Friends! would you live? some pills then take
   When head and stomack both do ake.

[MAY]

White Coates! whom choose you! whom you list:
   Some Ana-tolleratorist:
Wolves, lambs, hens, foxes to agree
   By setting all opinion-free:
If Blue-coates do not this prevent,
   Hobgoblins will be insolent.

⑥ *Humor in the Colonies*

[JUNE]

Who dig'd this spring of Gardens here,
    Whose mudded streames at last run cleare?
But why should we such water drink?
    Give loosers what they list to think,
Yet know, one God, one Faith profest
    To be New-England's interest.

[JULY]

The wooden Birds are now in sight,
    Whose voices roare, whose wings are white,
Whose mawes are fill'd with hose and shooes,
    With wine, cloth, sugar, salt and newes;
When they have eas'd their stomacks here,
    They cry, farewell untill next yeare.

[AUGUST]

Many this month I do fore-see
    Together by the eares will bee:
Indian and English in the field
    To one another will not yield.
Some weeks continue will this fray,
    Till they be carted all away.

[SEPTEMBER]

Four heads should meet and counsell have,
    The chickens from the kite to save,
The idle drones away to drive,
    The little Bees to keep i'th hive.
How honey may be brought to these
    By making fish to dance on trees.

[OCTOBER]

If discontented Bellies shall
    Wish that the highest now might fall:
Their wish fulfilled they shall see,
    Whenas within the woods they bee.
Poor Tinker think'st our shrubs will sing:
    The Bramble here shall be our King.

[NOVEMBER]

None of the wisest now will crave
    To know what winter we shall have.
It shall be milde, let such be told,
    If that it be not over cold.
Nor over cold shall they it see,
    If very temperate it bee.

[DECEMBER]

It may be now some enemy—
    Not seen, but felt, will make you fly.
Where is it best then to abide:
    I think close by the fire side.
If you must fight it out i'th field,
    Your hearts let woollen breast-plates shield.

[JANUARY]

Great bridges shall be made alone,
    Without ax, timber, earth or stone,
Of crystal metall, like to glasse;
    Such wondrous works soon come to passe.
If you may then have such a way,
    The Ferry-man you need not pay.

8 *Humor in the Colonies*

[FEBRUARY]

Our Lillies which refus'd to spin
  All winter past, shall now begin
To feel the lash of such a Dame,
  Whom some call Idleness by name.
Excepting such who all this time
  Had reason good against my rime.

Epitaph Written 1728

Benjamin Franklin

The Body of
B Franklin Printer,
(Like the Cover of an old Book
Its Contents torn out
And stript of its Lettering & Gilding)
Lies here, Food for Worms.
But the Work shall not be lost;
For it will, (as he believ'd) appear once more,
In a new and more elegant Edition
Revised and corrected,
By the Author.

9

The Flies

Benjamin Franklin

To Madame He—s

The flies of the apartments of M. F—n request permission to present their respects to Mme. H—s, and to express in their best language their gratitude for the protection that she has kindly wished to give them,

Bizz izzzz ouizz a ouizzzz izzzzzzzz, etc.

We have lived a long time under the hospitable roof of the said good man F—n. He has given us lodging gratis; we have also eaten and drunk the whole year at his expense without its having cost us anything. Often when his friends have used up a bowl of his punch, he has left a sufficient quantity to intoxicate a hundred of us other flies. We have drunk freely there, and after that we have made our sallies, our circles and our cotillions very prettily in the air of his chamber, and we have gaily consummated our little amours under his [very] nose. Finally, we should have been the most happy people in the world if he had not permitted to remain over the top of his wainscoting a number of our declared enemies, who stretched their tiny web threads in order to capture us, and who would destroy us without pity. People of temperament and subtle and fierce, abominable crowd! You, very excellent lady—had the goodness to order that all these assassins with their habitations and their snares be swept; and your orders (as they always must be) have been immediately executed. Since this time we live happily, and we enjoy the beneficence of the said good man F——n without fear.

There only remains one thing for us to wish in order to assure the permanence of our good fortune; permit us to say it

Bizz izzzz ouizz a ouizzzz izzzzzzz, etc.

Henceforth it is your responsibility to see that [yours and his] be made into a single household.

Epitaph On a Patient Killed by a Cancer Quack

Lemuel Hopkins

Here lies a fool flat on his back,
The victim of a Cancer Quack;
Who lost his money and his life,
By plaster, caustic, and by knife.
The case was this—a pimple rose,
South-east a little of his nose;
Which daily redden'd and grew bigger,
As too much drinking gave it vigour:
A score of gossips soon ensure
Fully three score diff'rent modes of cure;
But yet the full-fed pimple still
Defied all petticoated skill;
When fortune led him to peruse
A hand-bill in the weekly news;
Sign'd by six fools of diff'rent sorts,
All cur'd of cancers made of warts;
Who recommended, with due submission,
This cancer-monger as magician;
Fear wing'd his flight to find the quack,
And prove his cancer-curing knack;
But on his way he found another,—
A second advertising brother:
But as much like him as an owl
Is unlike every handsome fowl;

Whose fame has rais'd as broad a fog,
And of the two the greater hog:
Who us'd a still more magic plaster,
That sweat forsooth, and cur'd the faster.
This doctor view'd with moony eyes,
And scowl'd up face, the pimple's size;
Then christen'd it in solemn answer,
And cried, "This pimple's name is CANCER."
"But courage, friend, I see you're pale,
"My sweating plasters never fail;
"I've sweated hundreds out with ease,
"With roots as long as maple trees;
"And never failed in all my trials—
"Behold these samples here in vials!
"Preserv'd to shew my wond'rous merits,
"Just as my liver is—in spirits.
"For twenty joes the cure is done—"
The bargain struck, the plaster on,
Which gnaw'd the cancer at its leisure,
And pained his face above all measure.
But still the pimple spread the faster,
And swell'd, like toad that meets disaster.
Thus foil'd, the doctor gravely swore,
It was a right rose-cancer sore;
Then stuck his probe beneath the beard,
And shew'd them where the leaves appear'd;
And rais'd the patient's drooping spirits,
By praising up the plaster's merits.—
Quoth he, "The roots now scarcely stick—
"I'll fetch her out like crab or tick;
"And make it rendezvous, next trial,
"With six more plagues, in my old vial."
Then purg'd him pale with jalap drastic,

And next applies th' infernal caustic.
But yet, this semblance bright of hell
Serv'd but to make the patient yell;
And, gnawing on with fiery pace,
Devour'd one broadside of his face—
"Courage, 'tis done," the doctor cried,
And quick th' incision knife applied:
That with three cuts made such a hole,
Out flew the patient's tortur'd soul!

Go, readers, gentle, eke and simple,
If you have wart, or corn, or pimple;
To quack infallible apply;
Here's room enough for you to lie.
His skill triumphant still prevails,
For DEATH'S a cure that never fails.

Yankee Doodle
A Patriotic Song

Father and I went down to camp,
    Along with Captain Tooding,
And there we see the men and boys,
    As thick as hasty pudding.
        Yankee Doodle, keep it up;
          Yankee Doodle dandy,
        Mind the music and the step,
          And with the girls be handy.

And there we see a thousand men,
    As rich as Squire David,
And what they wasted every day,
    I wish it could be saved.

The 'lasses they eat every day,
    Would keep a house a winter;
They have as much that I'll be bound
    They eat it when they've a mind to.

And there we see a swamping gun,
    Large as a log of maple,
Upon a deuced little cart,
    A load for father's cattle.

16 *Humor in the Colonies*

And every time they shoot it off
   It takes a horn of powder,
And makes a noise like father's gun,
   Only a nation louder.

I went as nigh to one myself
   As Siah's underpinning;
And father went as nigh again,
   I thought the deuce was in him.

Cousin Simon grew so bold,
   I thought he would have cock'd it,
It scared me so, I shrink'd it off,
   And hung by father's pocket.

And Captain Davis had a gun,
   He kind of clapt his hand on't,
And stuck a crooked stabbing iron
   Upon the little end on't.

And there I see a pumpkin-shell
   As big as mother's bason,
And every time they touch'd it off,
   They scamper'd like the nation.

I see a little barrel too,
   The heads were made of leather,
They knock'd upon't with little clubs,
   And call'd the folks together.

There was Captain Washington,
   Upon a slapping stallion,

A giving orders to his men—
   I guess there was a million.

And then the feathers on his hat,
   They look'd so tarnal fina,
I wanted pockily to get,
   To give to my Jemima.

And then they'd fife away like fun,
   And play on cornstalk fiddles;
And some had ribbons red as blood,
   All wound about their middles.

The troopers, too, would gallop up,
   And fire right in our faces;
It scar'd me almost half to death,
   To see them run such races.

Old Uncle Sam came there to change
   Some pancakes and some onions,
For 'lasses-cakes to carry home
   To give his wife and young ones.

But I can't tell you half I see,
   They kept up such a smother;
So I took my hat off, made a bow,
   And scampered home to mother.

Joe Miller's Jokes

A scholar meeting a person said to him, "I am surprised to see you. I was told you were dead."

To which the person replied, "Now you see I am alive."

The scholar thought a moment, then he said, "Perhaps so. But the man who told me has a better reputation than you for telling the truth."

A gentleman that bore a spleen to another met him in the street and boxed his ears. The struck man asked, "Was that a jest or were you in earnest?"

The gentleman replied, "It was in earnest."

"I am glad of that," said the other man, "for if it had been done in jest, I would have been very angry."

A parson, seeing his son play roguish tricks, said, "Look! Did you ever see me do things like that when I was a boy?"

John-a-Noaks was driving his cart toward Croydon, and growing tired, he fell asleep in it. While he was sleeping someone unhitched his two horses and went away with them. When he awoke and found his horses missing, he exclaimed, "Either I am John-a-Noaks or I am not John-a-Noaks. If I am John-a-Noaks, then I have lost two horses. If I am not John-a-Noaks, then I have found a cart."

At a trial for assault a carpenter was being browbeaten by a counselor. "What distance were you from the parties when you saw the defendant strike the plaintiff?" he was asked.

"Exactly four feet, five and a half inches," replied the carpenter.

"How is it possible," asked the counsel, "for you to be so very exact as to the distance?"

"To tell the truth," said the carpenter, "I thought perhaps some fool would ask me, and so I measured the distance."

Two persons who had been formerly acquainted but had not seen each other in a great while met on the road and one asked the other how he did.

"I've been married since I saw you." said the first.

"That is well," said the second.

"Not so well either," said the first, "for I married a shrew."

"That is ill," said the second.

"Not so ill either," said the first, "for she brought me two thousand pounds."

"That is well," said the second.

"Not so well either," said the first, "for I spent it all on sheep, and they died of the rot."

"That is ill indeed," said the second.

"Not so ill either," said the first, "for I sold the skins for more money than the sheep cost."

"That was well indeed," said the second.

"Not so well either," said the first, "for I spent the money on a house and it burned down."

"That was very ill," said the second.

"Not so ill either," said the first, "for my wife was in it."

An Irish lawyer, having occasion to go to dinner, left these directions written and put in the keyhole of his chamber door: "I am gone to the Elephant and Castle, where you shall find me. If you can't read this note, carry it to the stationer's and he will read it for you."

Mr. G—n, the surgeon, being sent for by a gentleman who had received a slight wound, gave order to his servant to go home with all haste imaginable and fetch a certain plaster. The patient turned a little pale. "Sir," said he, "is there any danger?"

"Indeed there is," answered the surgeon. "If the fellow doesn't hurry, the wound will heal before he returns."

A melting sermon being preached in a country church, all fell a-weeping—all but one. When he was asked why he did not weep with the rest, he replied, "I belong to another parish."

A soldier was bragging before Caesar about the many wounds he had received in the face. Caesar, knowing him to be a coward, said, "Better take heed the next time you run away. Don't look back."

A lap dog belonging to a fashionable lady bit a piece out of a male visitor's leg. "Oh, dear," said the lady. "I hope it doesn't make the poor creature sick."

"I am glad to see you better," said his surgeon to the actor Samuel Foote. "You followed my prescription, of course."

"On the contrary," said Foote. "Had I followed your prescription I would have broken my neck."

"Broken your neck?" exclaimed the surgeon. "How so?"

"Absolutely," said Foote. "I threw the prescription out of my third-story window."

2.

1781-1860

Frontier Humor

The Heroic People of Windham—Samuel A. Peters
Wouter Van Twiller—Washington Irving
The Coon-Skin Trick—Davy Crockett
The Big Bear of Arkansas—T.B. Thorpe
Abe Lincoln's Jokes
Yankee Exaggerations

Introduction

It was not only the explorers who, after the Revolutionary War, pushed at the frontier. Farmers and fishermen, woodsmen and river boatmen, horse dealers and mule drivers, all mastered somehow the forces of nature so often aligned against them as they travelled westward. Though nearly always lonely, pioneer men and women survived both journey and the early days of homesteading. Their success engendered an exuberance that gave a fresh dimension to the humor of the day. The prairie, backwoods, and wilderness way of life stimulated new words and new stories, each more exaggerated than the last.

Communities grew as more and more settlers from the East found land to their liking. In a way that is peculiarly American, laughter between new neighbors in what had been unpopulated territory served to unify them. Men now exchanged tales and jokes over cracker barrels in the country store, women over the quilting bee.

Americans now began to indulge in practical jokes. And wit became more subtle, as illustrated by the kind of story Lincoln loved to tell. Comedies were demanded of actors travelling between settlements, and the popular newspapers were those including jokes or comical tidbits culled from the day's news.

People were revolting against rigidly polite behavior, as practiced on the old continent, or by highbrow English, French, and Spanish society on the new. The backwoodsman in particular mocked at rules, and instead idealized the tough, shrewd swashbuckler who adored foolishness and abhored fools.

The Heroic People of Windham

Samuel A. Peters

Windham the second county in the ancient kingdom of Sassacus, or colony of Saybrook, is hilly; but, the soil being rich, has excellent butter, cheese, hemp, wheat, Indian corn, and horses. Its towns are twelve.

Windham resembles Rumford, and stands on Winnomantic river. Its meeting-house is elegant, and has a steeple, bell, and clock. Its court-house is scarcely to be looked upon as an ornament. The township forms four parishes, and is ten miles square.

Strangers are very much terrified at the hideous noise made on summer evenings by the vast number of frogs in the brooks and ponds. There are about thirty different voices among them; some of which resemble the bellowing of a bull. The owls and whippoorwills complete the rough concert, which may be heard several miles. Persons accustomed to such serenades are not disturbed by them at their proper stations; but one night, in July, 1758, the frogs of an artificial pond, three miles square, and about five from Windham, finding the water dried up, left the place in a body, and marched, or rather hopped, towards Winnomantic river. They were under the necessity of taking the road and going through the town, which they entered about midnight. The bull frogs were the leaders, and the pipers followed without number. They filled a road 40 yards wide for four miles in length, and were for several hours in passing through the town, unusually clamorous. The inhabitants were equally perplexed and frightened: some expected to find an army of French and Indians; others feared an earthquake, and dissolution of nature. The consternation was universal. Old and young, male and female, fled naked from their beds with worse shriekings than those of the frogs. The event was fatal to several women. The men, after a flight of half a mile, in which they met with many broken shins, finding no enemies in pursuit of them, made a halt, and summoned resolution enough to venture back to their wives and children; when they distinctly heard from the enemy's camp these words, *Wight, Hilderken, Dier, Tete*. This last they thought meant *treaty*; and plucking up courage, they sent a triumvirate to capitulate with the supposed French and Indians. These three men approached in their shirts, and begged to speak with the General; but it being dark, and no answer given, they were sorely agitated for some time betwixt hope and fear; at length, however, they discovered that the dreaded inimical army was an army of thirsty frogs, going to the river for a little water.

Such an incursion was never known before nor since; and yet the people of Windham have been ridiculed for their timidity on this occasion. I verily believe an army under the Duke of Marlborough, would, under like circumstances, have acted no better than they did.

Wouter Van Twiller
Washington Irving

It was in the year of our Lord 1629 that Mynheer
Wouter Van Twiller was appointed governor of the
province of Nieuw Nederlandts, under the commission
and control of their High Mightinesses the Lords States
General of the United Netherlands, and the privileged
West India Company.

This renowned old gentleman arrived at New Amsterdam in the merry month of June, the sweetest
month in all the year; when dan Apollo seems to dance
up the transparent firmament,—when the robin, the
thrush, and a thousand other wanton songsters make
the woods to resound with amorous ditties, and the
luxurious little bob-lincoln revels among the clover-
blossoms of the meadows,—all which happy coinci-
dence persuaded the old dames of New Amsterdam,
who were skilled in the art of foretelling events, that
this was to be a happy and prosperous administration.

The renowned Wouter (or Walter) Van Twiller was
descended from a long line of Dutch burgomasters,
who had successively dozed away their lives and grown
fat upon the bench of magistracy in Rotterdam; and
who had comported themselves with such singular
wisdom and propriety, that they were never either
heard or talked of—which, next to being universally

applauded, should be the object of ambition of all magistrates and rulers. There are two opposite ways by which some men make a figure in the world; one, by talking faster than they think, and the other, by holding their tongues and not thinking at all. By the first, many a smatterer acquires the reputation of a man of quick parts; by the other, many a dunderpate, like the owl, the stupidest of birds, comes to be considered the very type of wisdom. This, by the way, is a casual remark, which I would not, for the universe, have it thought I apply to Governor Van Twiller. It is true he was a man shut up within himself, like an oyster, and rarely spoke, except in monosyllables; but then it was allowed he seldom said a foolish thing. So invincible was his gravity that he was never known to laugh or even to smile through the whole course of a long and prosperous life. Nay, if a joke were uttered in his presence, that set light-minded hearers in a roar, it was observed to throw him into a state of perplexity. Sometimes he would deign to inquire into the matter, and when, after much explanation, the joke was made as plain as a pike-staff, he would continue to smoke his pipe in silence, and at length, knocking out the ashes, would exclaim, "Well, I see nothing in all that to laugh about."

With all his reflective habits, he never made up his mind on a subject. His adherents accounted for this by the astonishing magnitude of his ideas. He conceived every subject on so grand a scale that he had not room in his head to turn it over and examine both sides of it. Certain it is, that if any matter were propounded to him on which ordinary mortals would rashly determine at first glance, he would put on a vague, mysterious look, shake his capacious head, smoke some time in profound silence, and at length observe, that "he had his doubts about the matter"; which gained him the reputation of a man slow of belief and not easily imposed upon. What is more, it gained him a lasting name; for to this habit of the mind has been attributed his surname of Twiller; which is said to be a corruption of the original Twijfler, or, in plain English, *Doubter*.

The person of this illustrious old gentleman was formed and proportioned as though it had been moulded by the hands of some cunning Dutch statuary, as a model of majesty and lordly grandeur. He was exactly five feet six inches in height, and six feet five inches in circumference. His head was a perfect sphere, and of such stupendous dimensions, that Dame Nature, with all her sex's ingenuity, would have been puzzled to construct a neck capable of supporting it; wherefore she wisely declined the attempt, and settled it firmly on the top of his backbone, just between the shoulders. His body was oblong, and particularly capacious at bottom; which was wisely ordered by Providence, seeing that he was a man of sedentary habits, and very averse to the idle labor of walking. His legs were short, but sturdy in proportion to the weight they had to sustain; so that when erect he had not a little the appearance of a beer barrel on skids. His face, that infallible index of the mind, presented a vast expanse, unfurrowed by those lines and angles which disfigure the human countenance with what is termed expression. Two small gray eyes twinkled feebly in the midst, like two stars of lesser magnitude in a hazy firmament, and his full-fed cheeks, which seemed to have taken toll of everything that went into his mouth, were curiously mottled and streaked with dusty red, like a spitzenberg apple.

His habits were as regular as his person. He daily took his four stated meals, appropriating exactly an hour to each; he smoked and doubted eight hours, and he slept the remaining twelve of the four-and-twenty. Such was the renowned Wouter Van Twiller,—a true philosopher, for his mind was either elevated above, or tranquilly settled below, the cares and perplexities of this world. He had lived in it for years, without feeling the least curiosity to know whether the sun revolved round it, or it round the sun; and he had watched, for at least half a century, the smoke curling from his pipe to the ceiling, without once troubling his head with any of those numerous theories by which a philosopher would have perplexed his brain, in accounting for its rising above the surrounding atmosphere.

In his council he presided with great state and solemnity. He sat in a huge chair of solid oak, hewn in the celebrated forest of the Hague, fabricated by an experienced timmerman of Amsterdam, and curiously carved about the arms and feet into exact imitations of gigantic eagle's claws. Instead of a scepter, he swayed a long Turkish pipe, wrought with jasmin and amber, which had been presented to a stadtholder of Holland at the conclusion of a treaty with one of the petty Barbary powers. In this stately chair would he sit, and this magnificent pipe would he smoke, shaking his right knee with a constant motion, and fixing his eye for hours together upon a little print of Amsterdam, which hung in a black frame against the opposite wall of the council-chamber. Nay, it has even been said, that when any deliberation of extraordinary length and intricacy was on the carpet, the renowned Wouter would shut his eyes for full two hours at a time, that he might not be disturbed by external objects; and at such times the internal commotion of his mind was evinced by certain regular guttural sounds, which his admirers declared were merely the noise of conflict, made by his contending doubts and opinions.

It is with infinite difficulty I have been enabled to collect these biographical anecdotes of the great man under consideration. The facts respecting him were so scattered and vague, and divers of them so questionable in point of authenticity, that I have had to give up the search after many, and decline the admission of still more, which would have tended to heighten the coloring of his portrait.

I have been the more anxious to delineate fully the person and habits of Wouter Van Twiller, from the consideration that he was not only the first, but also the best governor that ever presided over this ancient and respectable province; and so tranquil and benevolent was his reign, that I do not find throughout the whole of it a single instance of any offender being brought to punishment,—a most indubitable sign of a merciful governor, and a case unparalleled, excepting in the reign of the illustrious King Log, from whom, it is hinted, the renowned Van Twiller was a lineal descendant.

The very outset of the career of this excellent magistrate was distinguished by an example of legal acumen, that gave flattering presage of a wise and equitable administration. The morning after he had been installed in office, and at the moment that he was making his breakfast from a prodigious earthen dish, filled

with milk and Indian pudding, he was interrupted by
the appearance of Wandle Schoonhoven, a very important old burgher of New Amsterdam, who complained
bitterly of one Barent Bleecker, inasmuch as he refused
to come to a settlement of accounts, seeing that there
was a heavy balance in favor of the said Wandle. Governor Van Twiller, as I have already observed, was a
man of few words; he was likewise a mortal enemy to
multiplying writings—or being disturbed at his breakfast. Having listened attentively to the statement of
Wandle Schoonhoven, giving an occasional grunt, as
he shoveled a spoonful of Indian pudding into his
mouth,—either as a sign that he relished the dish, or
comprehended the story,—he called unto him his constable, and pulling out of his breeches-pocket a huge
jack-knife, dispatched it after the defendant as a sum-
mons, accompanied by his tobacco-box as a warrant.

This summary process was as effectual in those simple days as was the seal-ring of the great Haroun Alras-
chid among the true believers. The two parties being
confronted before him, each produced a book of accounts, written in a language and character that would
have puzzled any but a High-Dutch commentator, or a
learned decipherer of Egyptian obelisks. The sage
Wouter took them one after the other, and having
poised them in his hands, and attentively counted over
the number of leaves, fell straightway into a very great
doubt, and smoked for half an hour without saying a
word; at length, laying his finger beside his nose, and
shutting his eyes for a moment, with the air of a man
who has just caught a subtle idea by the tail, he slowly
took his pipe from his mouth, puffed forth a column of
tobacco-smoke, and with marvelous gravity and sol-

emnity pronounced, that, having carefully counted over the leaves and weighed the books, it was found, that one was just as thick and heavy as the other: therefore, it was the final opinion of the court that the accounts were equally balanced: therefore, Wandle should give Barent a receipt, and Barent should give Wandle a receipt, and the constable should pay the costs.

This decision, being straightway made known, diffused general joy throughout New Amsterdam, for the people immediately perceived that they had a very wise and equitable magistrate to rule over them. But its happiest effect was, that not another lawsuit took place throughout the whole of his administration; and the office of constable fell into such decay, that there was not one of those losel scouts known in the province for many years. I am the more particular in dwelling on this transaction, not only because I deem it one of the most sage and righteous judgments on record, and well worth the attention of modern magistrates, but because it was a miraculous event in the history of the renowned Wouter—being the only time he was ever known to come to a decision in the whole course of his life.

The Coon-Skin Trick

Davy Crockett

While on the subject of election matters, I will just relate a little anecdote about myself, which will show the people to the East how we manage these things on the frontiers. It was when I first run for Congress; I was then in favor of the Hero (Andrew Jackson), for he had chalked out his course so sleek in his letter to the Tennessee legislature that, like Sam Patch, says I, "There can be no mistake in him," and so I went ahead. No one dreamt about the monster and the deposits at that time, and so, as I afterward found, many like myself were taken in by these fair promises, which were worth about as much as a flash in the pan when you have a fair shot at a fat bear.

But I am losing sight of my story. Well, I started off to the Cross Roads dressed in my hunting shirt, and my rifle on my shoulder. Many of our constituents had assembled there to get a taste of the quality of the candidates at orating. Job Snelling, a gander-shanked Yankee, who had been caught somewhere about Plymouth Bay, and been shipped to the West with a cargo of codfish and rum, erected a large shantee, and set up shop for the occasion. A large posse of the voters had assembled before I arrived, and my opponent had already made considerable headway with his speechifying and his treating, when they spied me about a rifle shot from camp, sauntering along as if I was not a party in business. "There comes Crockett," cried one. "Let us hear the colonel," cried another; and so I mounted the stump that had been cut down for the occasion, and began to bushwack in the most approved style.

I had not been up long before there was such an uproar in the crowd that I could not hear my own voice, and some of my constituents let me know that they could not listen to me on such a dry subject as the welfare of the nation until they had something to drink, and that I must treat them. Accordingly I jumped down from the rostrum, and led the way to the shantee, followed by my constituents, shouting, "Huzza for Crockett!" and "Crockett forever!"

When we entered the shantee Job was busy dealing out his rum in a style that showed he was making a good day's work of it, and I called for a quart of the best; but the crooked critter returned no other answer than by pointing to a board over the bar, on which he had chalked in large letters, *"Pay to-day and trust to-morrow."* Now that idea brought me up all standing; it was a sort of cornering in which there was no back-out, for ready money in the West, in those times, was the shyest thing in all natur, and it was most particularly shy with me on that occasion.

The voters, seeing my predicament, fell off to the other side, and I was left deserted and alone, as the Government will be, when he no longer has any offices to bestow. I saw as plain as day that the tide of popular opinion was against me, and that unless I got some rum speedily I should lose my election as sure as there are snakes in Virginny; and it must be done soon, or

even burnt brandy wouldn't save me. So I walked away
from the shantee, but in another guess sort from the
way I entered it, for on this occasion I had no train
after me, and not a voice shouted, "Huzza for Crockett!" Popularity sometimes depends on a very small
matter indeed; in this particular it was worth a quart of
New England rum, and no more.

Well, knowing that a crisis was at hand, I struck
into the woods, with my rifle on my shoulder, my best
friend in time of need; and, as good fortune would have
it, I had not been out more than a quarter of hour
before I treed a fat coon, and in the pulling of a trigger
he lay dead at the foot of the tree. I soon whipped his
hairy jacket off his back, and again bent my steps
towards the shantee, and walked up to the bar, but not
alone, for this time I had half a dozen of my constituents at my heels. I threw down the coon-skin upon
the counter, and called for a quart, and Job, though
busy dealing out rum, forgot to point at his chalked
rules and regulations; for he knew that a coon was as
good a legal tender for a quart in the West as a New
York shilling any day in the year.

My constituents now flocked about me, and cried,
"Huzza for Crockett!" "Crockett forever!" and finding
the tide had taken a turn, I told them several yarns to
get them in a good humor; and having soon dispatched
the value of the coon, I went out and mounted the
stump without opposition, and a clear majority of the
voters followed me to hear what I had to offer for the
good of the nation. Before I was half through one of my
constituents moved that they would hear the balance of
my speech after they had washed down the first part
with some more of Job Snelling's extract of cornstalk

and molasses, and the question being put, it was carried unanimously. It wasn't considered necessary to tell
the yeas and nays, so we adjourned to the shantee, and
on the way I began to reckon that the fate of the nation
pretty much depended upon my shooting another
coon.

While standing at the bar, feeling sort of bashful
while Job's rules and regulations stared me in the face,
I cast down my eyes, and discovered one end of the
coon-skin sticking between the logs that supported the
bar. Job had slung it there in the hurry of business. I
gave it a sort of quick jerk, and it followed my hand as
natural as if I had been the rightful owner. I slapped it
on the counter, and Job, little dreaming that he was
barking up the wrong tree, shoved along another bot-
tle, which my constituents quickly disposed of with
good humor, for some of them saw the trick; and then
we withdrew to the rostrum to discuss the affairs of the
nation.

I don't know how it was, but the voters soon became
dry again, and nothing would do but we must adjourn
to the shantee; and as luck would have it, the coon-
skin was still sticking between the logs, as if Job had
flung it there on purpose to tempt me. I was not slow
in rising it to the counter, the rum followed, of course,
and I wish I may be shot if I didn't, before the day was
over, get ten quarts for the same identical skin, and
from a fellow, too, who in those parts was considered
as sharp as a steel trap and as bright as a pewter button.

This joke secured me my election, for it soon circulated like smoke among my constituents, and they
allowed, with one accord, that the man who could get
the whip hand of Job Snelling in fair trade, could

outwit Old Nick himself, and was the real grit for them in Congress. Job was by no means popular; he boasted of always being wide awake, and that any one who could take him in was free to do so, for he came from a stock that, sleeping or waking, had always one eye open, and the other not more than half closed. The whole family were geniuses. His father was the inventor of wooden nutmegs, by which Job said he might have made a fortune, if he had only taken out a patent and kept the business in his own hands; his mother, Patience, manufactured the first white oak pumpkin seeds of the mammoth kind, and turned a pretty penny the first season; and his aunt Prudence was the first to discover that corn husks, steeped into tobacco water, would make as handsome Spanish wrappers as ever came from Havana, and that oak leaves would answer all the purpose of filling, for no one could discover the difference except the man who smoked them, and then it would be too late to make a stir about it. Job himself bragged of having made some useful discoveries, the most profitable of which was the art of converting mahogany sawdust into cayenne pepper, which he said was a profitable and safe business; for the people have been so long accustomed to having dust thrown in their eyes that there wasn't much danger of being found out.

The way I got to the blind side of the Yankee merchant was pretty generally known before election day, and the result was that my opponent might as well have whistled jigs to a milestone as attempt to beat up for votes in that district. I beat him out and out, quite back into the old year, and there was scarce enough left of him, after the canvass was over, to make a small grease spot. He disappeared without even leaving a mark behind; and such will be the fate of Adam Huntsman, if there is a fair fight and no gouging.

After the election was over, I sent Snelling the price of the rum, but took good care to keep the fact from the knowledge of my constituents. Job refused the money, and sent me word that it did him good to be taken in occasionally, as it served to brighten his ideas; but I afterwards learnt when he found out the trick that had been played upon him, he put all the rum I had ordered in his bill against my opponent, who, being elated with the speeches he had made on the affairs of the nation, could not descend to examine into the particulars of a bill of a vendor of rum in the small way.

The Big Bear
of Arkansas

T. B. Thorpe

A steamboat on the Mississippi frequently, in making her regular trips, carries between places varying from one to two thousand miles apart; and as these boats advertise to land passengers and freight at "all intermediate landings," the heterogeneous character of the passengers of one of these up-country boats can scarcely be imagined by one who has never seen it with his own eyes. Starting from New Orleans in one of these boats, you will find yourself associated with men from every state in the Union, and from every portion of the globe; and a man of observation need not lack for amusement or instruction in such a crowd, if he will take the trouble to read the great book of character so favorably opened before him. Here may be seen jostling together the wealthy Southern planter, and the pedlar of tin-ware from New England—the Northern merchant, and the Southern jockey—a venerable bishop, and a desperate gambler—the land speculator, and the honest farmer—professional men of all creeds and characters—Wolvereens, Suckers, Hoosiers, Buckeyes, and Corncrackers, besides a "plentiful sprinkling" of the half-horse and half-alligator species of men, who are peculiar to "old Mississippi," and who appear to gain a livelihood simply by going up and

down the river. In the pursuit of pleasure or business, I
have frequently found myself in such a crowd.

On one occasion, when in New Orleans, I had occasion to take a trip of a few miles up the Mississippi,
and I hurried on board the well-known "high-
pressure-and-beat-every-thing" steamboat *Invincible*,
just as the last note of the last bell was sounding; and
when the confusion and bustle that is natural to a
boat's getting under way had subsided, I discovered
that I was associated in as heterogeneous a crowd as was
ever got together. As my trip was to be of a few hours'
duration only, I made no endeavors to become acquainted with my fellow passengers, most of whom
would be together many days. Instead of this, I took
out of my pocket the "latest paper," and more critically than usual examined its contents; my fellow passengers at the same time disposed of themselves in
little groups. While I was thus busily employed in
reading, and my companions were more busily still
employed in discussing such subjects as suited their
humors best, we were startled most unexpectedly by a
loud Indian whoop, uttered in the "social hall," that
part of the cabin fitted off for a bar; then was to be
heard a loud crowing, which would not have continued
to have interested us—such sounds being quite common in that *place of spirits*—had not the hero of these
windy accomplishments stuck his head into the cabin
and hallooed out, "Hurra for the Big Bar of Arkansaw!" and then might be heard a confused hum of
voices, unintelligible, save in such broken sentences as
"horse," "screamer," "lightning is slow," &c. As
might have been expected, this continued interruption
attracted the attention of every one in the cabin; all

conversation dropped, and in the midst of this surprise the "Big Bar" walked into the cabin, took a chair, put his feet on the stove, and looking back over his shoulder, passed the general and familiar salute of "Strangers, how are you?" He then expressed himself as much at home as if he had been at "the Forks of Cypress," and "prehaps a little more so." Some of the company at this familiarity looked a little angry, and some astonished; but in a moment every face was wreathed in a smile. There was something about the intruder that won the heart on sight. He appeared to be a man enjoying perfect health and contentment: his eyes were as sparkling as diamonds, and good-natured to simplicity. Then his perfect confidence in himself was irresistibly droll. "Prehaps," said he, "gentlemen," running on without a person speaking, "prehaps you have been to New Orleans often; I never made *the first visit before*, and I don't intend to make another in a crow's life. I am thrown away in that ar place, and useless, that ar a fact. Some of the gentlemen thar called me *green*—well, prehaps I am, said I, *but I arn't so at home*; and if I ain't off my trail much, the heads of them perlite chaps themselves weren't much the hardest; for according to my notion, they were *real know-nothings*, green as a pumpkin vine—couldn't, in farming, I'll bet, raise a crop of turnips: and as for shooting, they'd miss a barn if the door was swinging, and that, too, with the best rifle in the country. And then they talked to me 'bout hunting, and laughed at my calling the principal game in Arkansaw poker, and high-low-jack. 'Prehaps,' said I, 'you prefer chickens and rolette'; at this they laughed harder than ever, and asked me if I lived in the woods, and didn't know what *game* was? At this I rather think I laughed. 'Yes,' I roared, and says, 'Strangers, if you'd asked me *how we got our meat* in Arkansaw, I'd a told you at once, and given you a list of varmints that would make a caravan, beginning with the bar, and ending off with the cat; that's *meat* though, not game.' Game, indeed that's what city folks call it; and with them it means chippen-birds and shite-pokes; maybe such trash live in my diggins, but I arn't noticed them yet: a bird any way is too trifling. I never did shoot at but one, and I'd never forgiven myself for that, had it weighed less than forty pounds. I wouldn't draw a rifle on any thing less than that; and when I meet with another wild turkey of the same weight I will drap him."

"A wild turkey weighing forty pounds!" exclaimed twenty voices in the cabin at once.

"Yes, strangers, and wasn't it a whopper? You see, the thing was so fat that it couldn't fly far; and then he fell out of the tree, after I shot him, on striking the ground he bust open behind, and the way the pound gobs of tallow rolled out of the opening was perfectly beautiful."

"Where did all that happen?" asked a cynical-looking Hoosier.

"Happen! happened in Arkansaw: where else could it have happened, but in the creation state, the finishing-up country—a state where the *sile* runs down to the centre of the 'arth, and government gives you a title to every inch of it? Then its airs—just breathe them, and they will make you snort like a horse. It's a state without a fault, it is."

"Excepting mosquitoes," cried the Hoosier.

"Well, stranger, except them; for it ar a fact that

they are rather *enormous* and do push themselves in somewhat troublesome. But, stranger, they never stick twice in the same place; and give them a fair chance for a few months, and you will get as much above noticing them as an alligator. They can't hurt my feelings, for they lay under the skin; and I never knew but one case of injury resulting from them, and that was to a Yankee: and they take worse to foreigners, any how, than they do to natives. But the way they used that fellow up! first they punched him until he swelled up and busted; then he su-per-a-ted, as the doctor called it, until he was as raw as beef; then he took the ager, owing to the warm weather, and finally he took a steamboat and left the country. He was the only man that ever took mosquitoes to heart that I know of. But mosquitoes is natur, and I never find fault with her. If they ar large, Arkansaw is large, her varmints ar large, her trees ar large, her rivers ar large, and a small mosquito would be of no more use in Arkansaw than preaching in a cane-brake."

This knock-down argument in favor of big mosquitoes used the Hoosier up, and the logician started on a new track, to explain how numerous bear were in his "diggins," where he represented them to be "about as plenty as blackberries, and a little plentifuler."

Upon the utterance of this assertion, a timid little man near me inquired if the bear in Arkansaw ever attacked the settlers in numbers.

"No," said our hero, warming with the subject, "no, stranger, for you see it ain't the natur of bar to go in droves; but the way they squander about in pairs and single ones is edifying. And then the way I hunt them the old black rascals know the crack of my gun as well as they know a pig's squealing. They grow thin in our parts, it frightens them so, and they do take the noise dreadfully, poor things. That gun of mine is a perfect *epidemic among bar*; if not watched closely, it will go off as quick on a warm scent as my dog Bowie-knife will: and then that dog—whew! why the fellow thinks that the world is full of bar, he finds them so easy. It's lucky he don't talk as well as think; for with his natural modesty, if he should suddenly learn how much he is acknowledged to be ahead of all other dogs in the universe, he would be astonished to death in two minutes. Strangers, the dog knows a bar's way as well as a horse-jockey knows a woman's: he always barks at the right time, bites at the exact place, and whips without getting a scratch. I never could tell whether he was made expressly to hunt bar, or whether bar was made expressly for him to hunt: any way, I believe they were ordained to go together as naturally as Squire Jones says a man and woman is, when he moralizes in marrying a couple. In fact, Jones once said, said he, 'Marriage according to law is a civil contract of divine origin; it's common to all countries as well as Arkansaw, and people take to it as naturally as Jim Doggett's Bowie-knife takes to bar.' "

"What season of the year do your hunts take place?" inquired a gentlemanly foreigner, who, from some peculiarities of his baggage, I suspected to be an Englishman, on some hunting expedition, probably at the foot of the Rocky Mountains.

"The season for bar hunting, stranger," said the man of Arkansaw, "is generally all the year round, and the hunts take place about as regular. I read in history that varmints have their fat season, and their lean season. That is not the case in Arkansaw, feeding as they do upon the *spontenacious* production of the sile, they have one continued fat season the year round: though in winter things in this way is rather more greasy than in summer, I must admit. For that reason bar with us run in warm weather, but in winter, they only waddle. Fat, fat! it's an enemy to speed; it tames everything that has plenty of it. I have seen wild turkeys, from its influence, as gentle as chickens. Run a bar in this fat condition, and the way it improves the critter for eating is amazing; it sort of mixes the ile up with the meat, until you can't tell t'other from which. I've done this often. I recollect one perty morning in particular, of putting an old he fellow on the stretch, and considering the weight he carried, he run well. But the dogs soon tired him down, and when I came up with him wasn't he in a beautiful sweat—I might say fever; and then to see his tongue sticking out of his mouth a few feet, and his sides sinking and opening like a bellows, and his cheeks so fat he couldn't look cross. In this fix I blazed at him, and pitch me naked into a briar patch if the steam didn't come out of the bullet-hole ten foot in a straight line. The fellow, I reckon, was made on the high-pressure system, and the lead sort of bust his biler."

"That column of steam was rather curious, or else the bear must have been *warm*," observed the foreigner, with a laugh.

"Stranger, as you observe, that bar was WARM, and the blowing off of the steam show'd it, and also how hard the varmint had been run. I have no doubt if he had kept on two miles farther his insides would have been stewed; and I expect to meet with a varmint yet of extra bottom, who will run himself into a skinfull of bar's grease: it is possible, much onlikelier things have happened."

"Whereabouts are these bears so abundant?" inquired the foreigner, with increasing interest.

"Why, stranger, they inhabit the neighborhood of my settlement, one of the prettiest places on old Mississippi—a perfect location, and no mistake; a place that had some defects until the river made the 'cut-off' at 'Shirt-tail bend,' and that remedied the evil, as it brought my cabin on the edge of the river—a great advantage in wet weather, I assure you, as you can now roll a barrel of whiskey into my yard in high water from a boat, as easy as falling off a log. It's a great improvement, as toting it by land in a jug, as I used to do, *evaporated* it too fast, and it became expensive. Just stop with me, stranger, a month or two, a year if you like, and you will appreciate my place. I can give you plenty to eat; for beside hog and hominy, you can have bar-ham, and bar sausages, and a mattrass of bar-skins to sleep on, and a wildcat-skin, pulled off hull, stuffed with corn-shucks, for a pillow. That bed would put you to sleep if you had the rheumatics in every joint in your body. I call that ar bed a *quietus*. Then look at my land—the government ain' got another such a piece to dispose of. Such timber, and such bottom land, why you can't preserve any thing natural you plant in it unless you pick it young, things thar will grow out of shape so quick. I once planted in those diggins a few potatoes and beets: they took a fine start, and after that an ox team couldn't have kept them from growing. About that time I went off to old Kentuck on bisiness, and did not hear from them things in three months, when I accidentally stumbled on a fellow who had stopped at my place, with an idea of buying me out. 'How did you like things?' said I. 'Pretty well,' said he; 'the cabin is convenient, and the timber land is good; but that bottom land ain't worth the first red cent.' 'Why?' said I. ' 'Cause,' said he. ' 'Cause what?' said I. ' 'Cause it's full of cedar stumps and Indian mounds,' said he, *and it can't be cleared.*' 'Lord,' said I, 'them ar "cedar stumps" is beets, and them ar "Indian mounds" ar tater hills.' As I expected, the crop was overgrown and useless: the sile is too rich, *and planting in Arkansaw is dangerous*. I had a good-sized sow killed in that same bottom land. The old thief stole an ear of corn, and took it down where she slept at night to eat. Well, she left a grain or two on the ground, and lay down on them: before morning the corn shot up, and the percussion killed her dead. I don't plant any more; natur intended Arkansaw for a hunting ground, and I go according to natur."

The questioner who thus elicited the description of our hero's settlement, seemed to be perfectly satisfied, and said no more; but the "Big Bar of Arkansaw" rambled on from one thing to another with a volubility perfectly astonishing, occasionally disputing with those around him, particularly with a "live Sucker" from Illinois, who had the daring to say that our Arkansaw friend's stories "smelt rather tall."

Abe Lincoln's Jokes

Lincoln told of a long-legged young man who was fond of a farmer's daughter but her father objected to him. One day the hostile farmer came in the house with a shotgun while the young man was there. The young man jumped out the window and started running across the field where he scared up a rabbit. He caught up with the rabbit and yelled, "Get out of this field and let somebody run that knows how."

One time he was walking down a dusty road when a stranger driving a buggy came along. He asked the stranger, "Would you be kind enough to take my coat to town with you?" The man in the buggy said it was okay, "But how will you get your coat back again?" "Oh, that's easy. I'm going to stay right inside it."

One of Lincoln's stories is about the time he was a young lawyer and an opposing lawyer objected to a juror because he knew Mr. Lincoln. The judge over-ruled the objection. Lincoln then started to question the jurors to see if any of them knew his opponent. The judge overruled again and said to Lincoln, "The mere

SANTA FE HIGH SCHOOL
LIBRARY

fact that a juror knows your opponent does not disqualify him." "No, Your Honor," Lincoln replied, "but I am afraid some of the gentlemen may not know him and that would place me at a disadvantage."

When he was running for office his opponent told the audience that the first time he met Lincoln was in a store where he was selling whiskey. Lincoln replied by saying, "What he has said is true. I worked in a general store and I did sell many different kinds of goods including whiskey. But I remember that he was one of my best customers. Many is the time I stood on one side of the counter and sold whiskey to my opponent here on the other. The difference between us now is that I left my side of the counter but he never left his."

Lincoln was once asked how long a man's legs should be and replied: "I think a man's legs should be long enough to reach from his body to the ground."

One time Lincoln was feeling sorry for himself and decided he was the ugliest man in the world and that if he should ever see an uglier man he would shoot him on sight. Shortly thereafter he saw someone and said, "That's my man." He went home and got his gun and went looking for the man. He pointed the gun at the man. "Why Lincoln what have I done?" "I made an oath that if I ever saw an uglier man than myself I would shoot him." "Well, if I am uglier than you, fire away."

At one time he was trying to make a point with an opponent and asked him, "Now suppose we call a cow's tail a leg, how many legs would the cow have?" "Why five, of course." "No. You still have four. Simply calling a cow's tail a leg doesn't make it one."

He liked to tell the story of the little girl who had blocks with letters on them and one night before going to bed was playing with them. When she got to bed she decided to say her prayers, but was so sleepy that all she could say was, "Oh, Lord. I am so sleepy. I can't say my prayers. Here are the blocks and the letters; You spell it out."

One time someone came to the White House and complained that General Grant drank whiskey. Lincoln replied: "Find out what brand he uses so I can furnish the same brand to the rest of my generals."

He was disappointed with one of his generals during the Civil War and wrote him; "If you don't want to use the army I should like to borrow it awhile."

A foreign diplomat came in upon Lincoln while he was shining his shoes. "What, Mr. President, you shine your own shoes?" "Yes," answered Lincoln, "whose shoes do you shine?"

Yankee Exaggerations

A man from Virginia has grown so tall that hot soup freezes before it gets down to his stomach. There is a boy out west who grew so fast his shadow couldn't keep up with him. Another man out west is so tall that he has to stand on a ladder to shave himself.

There is a man in Ohio so short that he has to stand on his own head to kiss his wife.

They have a man in Mississippi so thin he makes no shadow at all and a rattlesnake struck at his leg six times in vain and retired in disgust. There is a man in Indiana so thin that when the sheriff was after him he crawled into his rifle barrel and hid.

There was this politician with a mouth so big that one of his opponents threatened to go and live in it if he didn't close it.

There is a man who had a nose so big that he couldn't blow it without using gunpowder.

There is a family in Ohio so lazy that it takes two of them to sneeze, one to throw his head back and the other to make the noise.

There is one man who has such a good disposition that he rents himself out in the summer to keep people cool.

There is a man out west so cheap that he stands on

one foot at a time, for fear that he'll wear out his shoes too quickly.

There is a grocer so cheap that when he sees a fly on his counter he holds him up by the legs and looks into the cracks of his feet to see that he hasn't been stealing sugar.

A shoemaker in Massachusetts said that he made so many pairs of shoes in one day that it took him two days to count them. And a mason in New Hampshire built so many miles of stone wall that it took him two days to get home again.

A man from Missouri is so successful as a fisherman that he can tie a hook and line to each foot and dive in the river and bring up a fish on each foot.

A Californian says that they have fireflies so large that they use them to cook by.

One winter a cow floated down the Mississippi on a piece of ice and caught such a cold that she yielded nothing but ice cream ever since. And one time snow-flakes fell so large in Oregon that the ladies put handles on them and used them for umbrellas.

Another time it rained so hard in Arkansas that people had to jump into the river to keep from drowning.

It is said that in some towns in the west it is so healthy that the folks have to shoot a man to start a cemetery.

There is this lake in Minnesota that is so clear that by looking into it you can see them making tea in China.

3.

1861-1919

A National Sense of Humor

Cartoon—F. M. Howarth

Cartoon—Hy Mayer

Comic Strip—Katzenjammer Kids

Cartoon—Charles Dana Gibson

Cartoon—Boardman Robinson

Cartoon—Clare Briggs

The Glorious Whitewasher—Mark Twain (Samuel L. Clemens)

A Patented Child—W. L. Alden

Zenobia's Infidelity—H. C. Bunner

His Pa Plays Jokes—George Peck

The Ransom of Red Chief—O. Henry

Jane—Booth Tarkington

Early American Gravestones

Introduction

This was a turbulent period. Millions of immigrants arrived in America to work in the factories or on the railroads. Cities grew huge and travel between them became easier with faster boats and the new trains. Former slaves, beginning a new life, worked at the side of the immigrants, and both contributed their own comic traditions, their own dialects.

No longer restricted to regional folklore, American humor began to develop something of a national style. Travelling theatre groups, minstrel shows, and variety acts could open in Buffalo one week and be in Chicago the next, and the comedy that was their stock-in-trade was seen and heard from coast to coast.

In the emerging national humor, tensions and animosities reflected different backgrounds, economic situations, beliefs, places of work, and tastes of the country at large: pioneer settler against immigrant, factory worker against farmer, a simpler and more democratic life against a more rigidly class-structured European way of living, north against south, east against west, or quite simply rich against poor.

By this time, Americans were travelling east as

well as west in search of happiness or professional fulfillment. A note of dissatisfaction was creeping into their now quite sophisticated humor. There was irony in it and bitterness, these moods illustrated in the writings of Mark Twain. And there was now that American invention, the comic strip, often relying on ethnic background or social class for its humor, while still keeping alive the old love of nonsense and playfulness.

I.

II.

III.

IV.

V.

AN ELEVATED PET

F. M. HOWARTH —1897

·HY MAYER HAS SOME FUN WITH SPAGHETTI, 1899.

MAMMA KATZENJAMMER
PLAYS A BOOMERANG TRICK.

But the Kids Get Spanked Just the Same.

Rudolph Dirks, "The Katzenjammer Kids," 1901.

"TWO STRIKES AND THE BASES FULL"

"FANNED OUT"

CHARLES DANA GIBSON   —1904

"What's the célebration about, M's Milligan?"
"Sure, me boy's comin' home today. He was sentenced to ten years in the penitentiary, but he's got three years off for good conduct."
"Ah! I wish *I* had a son like that!"

A HANDY MAN AROUND THE HOUSE

CLARE BRIGGS   —1917

The Glorious Whitewasher

Mark Twain
(Samuel L. Clemens)

Saturday morning was come, and all the summer world was bright and fresh, and brimming with life. There was a song in every heart; and if the heart was young the music issued at the lips. There was cheer in every face and a spring in every step. The locust trees were in bloom and the fragrance of the blossoms filled the air. Cardiff Hill, beyond the village and above it, was green with vegetation, and it lay just far enough away to seem a Delectable Land, dreamy, reposeful, and inviting.

Tom appeared on the sidewalk with a bucket of whitewash and a long-handled brush. He surveyed the fence, and all gladness left him and a deep melancholy settled down upon his spirit. Thirty yards of board fence nine feet high. Life to him seemed hollow, and existence but a burden. Sighing he dipped his brush and passed it along the topmost plank; repeated the operation; did it again; compared the insignificant whitewashed streak with the far-reaching continent of unwhitewashed fence, and sat down on a tree-box discouraged. Jim came skipping out at the gate with a tin pail, and singing "Buffalo Gals." Bringing water from the town pump had always been hateful work in Tom's eyes, before, but now it did not strike him so. He remembered that there was company at the pump. White, mulatto, and Negro boys and girls were always there waiting their turns, resting, trading playthings, quarreling, fighting, skylarking. And he remembered that although the pump was only a hundred and fifty yards off, Jim never got back with a bucket of water under an hour—and even then somebody generally had to go after him. Tom said:

"Say, Jim, I'll fetch the water if you'll whitewash some."

Jim shook his head and said:

"Can't, Mars Tom. Ole missis, she tole me I got to go an' git dis water an' not stop folin' roun' wid anybody. She say she spec' Mars Tom gwin to ax me to whitewash, an' so she tole me go 'long an' 'tend to my own business—she 'lowed *she'd* 'tend to de whitewashin'."

"Oh, never you mind what she said, Jim. That's the way she always talks. Gimme the bucket—I won't be gone only a minute. *She* won't ever know."

"Oh, I dasn't, Mars Tom. Ole missis she'd take an' tar de head off'n me. 'Deed she would."

"*She!* She never licks anybody—whacks 'em over the head with her thimble—and who cares for that, I'd like to know. She talks awful, but talk don't hurt —anyways it don't if she don't cry. Jim, I'll give you a marvel. I'll give you a white alley!"

Jim began to waver.

"White alley, Jim! And it's a bully taw."

"My! Dat's a mighty gay marvel, *I* tell you! But Mars Tom, I's powerful 'fraid ole missis—"

"And besides, if you will I'll show you my sore toe."

Jim was only human—this attraction was too much

for him. He put down his pail, took the white alley, and bent over the toe with absorbing interest while the bandage was being unwound. In another moment he was flying down the street with his pail and a tingling rear, Tom was whitewashing with vigor, and Aunt Polly was retiring from the field with a slipper in her hand and triumph in her eye.

But Tom's energy did not last. He began to think of the fun he had planned for this day, and his sorrows multiplied. Soon the free boys would come tripping along on all sorts of delicious expeditions, and they would make a world of fun of him for having to work—the very thought of it burnt him like fire. He got out his worldly wealth and examined it—bits of toys, marbles, and trash; enough to buy an exchange of *work*, maybe, but not half enough to buy so much as half an hour of pure freedom. So he returned his straitened means to his pocket, and gave up the idea of trying to buy the boys. At this dark and hopeless moment an inspiration burst upon him! Nothing less than a great, magnificent inspiration.

He took up his brush and went tranquilly to work. Ben Rogers hove in sight presently—the very boy, of all boys, whose ridicule he had been dreading. Ben's gait was the hop-skip-and-jump—proof enough that his heart was light and his anticipations high. He was eating an apple, and giving a long, melodious whoop, at intervals, followed by a deep-toned ding-dong-dong, ding-dong-dong, for he was personating a steamboat. As he drew near, he slackened speed, took the middle of the street, leaned far over to starboard and rounded to ponderously and with laborious pomp and circumstance—for he was personating the *Big*

Missouri, and considered himself to be drawing nine feet of water. He was boat and captain and engine-bells combined, so he had to imagine himself standing on his own hurricane-deck giving the orders and executing them:

"Stop her sir! Ting-a-ling-ling!" The headway ran almost out and he drew up slowly toward the sidewalk.

"Ship up to back! Ting-a-ling-ling!" His arms straightened and stiffened down his sides.

"Set her back on the stabboard! Ting-a-ling-ling! Chow! ch-chow-wow! Chow!" His right hand, meantime, describing stately circles—for it was representing a forty-foot wheel.

"Let her go back on the labboard! Ting-a-ling-ling! Chow-ch-chow-chow!" The left hand began to describe circles.

"Stop the stabboard! Ting-a-ling-ling! Stop the labboard! Come ahead on the stabboard! Stop her! Let your outside turn over slow! Ting-a-ling-ling! Chow-ow-ow! Get out that head-line! *Lively* now! Come—out with your spring-line—what're you about there! Take a turn round that stump with the bight of it! Stand by that stage, now—let her go! Done with the engines, sir! Ting-a-ling-ling! *Sh't! sh't! sh't!*" (trying the gauge-cocks).

Tom went on whitewashing—paid no attention to the steamboat. Ben stared a moment and then said:

"Hi-*yi! You're* up a stump, ain't you!"

No answer. Tom surveyed his last touch with the eye of an artist, then he gave his brush another gentle sweep and surveyed the result, as before. Ben ranged up alongside of him. Tom's mouth watered for the apple, but he stuck to his work. Ben said.

Hello, old chap, you got to work, hey?"

Tom wheeled suddenly and said:

"Why, it's you, Ben! I warn't noticing."

"Say—I'm going in a-swimming, I am. Don't you wish you could? But of course you'd druther *work*—wouldn't you? Course you would!" Tom contemplated the boy a bit, and said:

"What do you call work?"

"Why, ain't *that* work?"

Tom resumed his whitewashing, and answered carelessly:

"Well, maybe it is, and maybe it ain't. All I know, is, it suits Tom Sawyer."

"Oh come, now, you don't mean to let on that you *like* it?"

The brush continued to move.

"Like it? Well, I don't see why I oughtn't to like it. Does a boy get a chance to whitewash a fence every day?"

That put the thing in a new light. Ben stopped nibbling his apple. Tom swept his brush daintily back and forth—stepped back to note the effect—added a touch here and there—criticized the effect again—Ben watching every move and getting more and more interested, more and more absorbed. Presently he said:

"Say, Tom, let *me* whitewash a little."

Tom considered, was about to consent; but he altered his mind:

"No—no—I reckon it wouldn't hardly do, Ben. You see, Aunt Polly's awful particular about this fence—right here on the street, you know—but if it was the back fence I wouldn't mind and *she* wouldn't. Yes, she's awful particular about this fence; it's got to be done very careful; I reckon there ain't one boy in a thousand, maybe two thousand, that can do it the way it's got to be done."

"No—is that so? Oh come, now—lemme just try. Only just a little—I'd let *you*, if you was me, Tom."

"Ben, I'd like to, honest injun; but Aunt Polly —well, Jim wanted to do it, but she wouldn't let him; Sid wanted to do it, and she wouldn't let Sid. Now don't you see how I'm fixed? If you was to tackle this fence and anything was to happen to it—"

"Oh, shucks, I'll be just as careful. Now lemme try. Say—I'll give you the core of my apple."

"Well, here— No, Ben, now don't. I'm afeard—"

"I'll give you *all* of it!"

Tom gave up the brush with reluctance in his face, but alacrity in his heart. And while the late steamer *Big Missouri* worked and sweated in the sun, the retired artist sat on a barrel in the shade close by, dangled his legs, munched his apple, and planned the slaughter of more innocents. There was no lack of material; boys happened along every little while; they came to jeer, but remained to whitewash. By the time Ben was fagged out, Tom had traded the next chance to Billy Fisher for a kite, in good repair; and when *he* played out, Johnny Miller bought in for a dead rat and a string to swing it with—and so on, and so on, hour after hour. And when the middle of the afternoon came, from being a poor poverty-stricken boy in the morning, Tom was literally rolling in wealth. He had besides the things before mentioned, twelve marbles, part of a jews'-harp, a piece of blue bottle-glass to look through, a spool cannon, a key that wouldn't unlock anything, a fragment of chalk, a glass stopper of a decanter, a tin soldier, a couple of tadpoles, six fire-crackers, a kitten with only one eye, a brass door-knob, a dog-collar—but no dog—the handle of a knife, four pieces of orange-peel, and a dilapidated old window-sash.

He had had a nice, good, idle time all the while —plenty of company—and the fence had three coats of whitewash on it! If he hadn't run out of whitewash, he would have bankrupted every boy in the village.

Tom said to himself that it was not such a hollow world, after all. He had discovered a great law of human action, without knowing it—namely, that in order to make a man or boy covet a thing, it is only necessary to make the thing difficult to attain. If he had been a great and wise philosopher, like the writer of this book, he would now have comprehended that Work consists of whatever a body is *obliged* to do, and that Play consists of whatever a body is not obliged to do. And this would help him to understand why con-structing artificial flowers or performing on a treadmill is work, while rolling tenpins or climbing Mont Blanc is only amusement. There are wealthy gentlemen in England who drive four-horse passenger-coaches twenty or thirty miles on a daily line, in the summer, because the privilege costs them considerable money; but if they were offered wages for the service, that would turn it into work and then they would resign.

The boy mused awhile over the substantial change which had taken place in his worldly circumstances, and then wended toward headquarters to report.

A Patented Child

W. L. Alden

The town of Sussex, Pennsylvania, has lately been profoundly stirred by an extraordinary and romantic lawsuit. The case was an entirely novel one, and no precedent bearing upon it is to be found in the common or statute law. While it is necessarily a matter of great interest to the legal profession, its romantic side cannot fail to attract the attention of persons of all ages and every kind of sex. In fact, it is destined to be one of the most celebrated cases in the annals of American jurisprudence.

Some time last winter a lady whom we will call Mrs. Smith, who kept a boarding-house in Sussex, took her little girl, aged four, with her to make a call on Mrs. Brown, her near neighbor. Mrs. Brown was busy in the kitchen, where she received her visitor with her usual cordiality. There was a large fire blazing in the stove, and while the ladies were excitedly discussing the new bonnet of the local Methodist minister's wife, the little girl incautiously sat down on the stove hearth. She was instantly convinced that the hearth was exceedingly hot, and on loudly bewailing the fact, was rescued by her mother and carried home for medical treatment. A few days later Mrs. Smith burst in great excitement into the room of a young law student, who was one of her boarders, and with tears and lamentations disclosed to him the fact that her child was indelibly branded with the legend, "Patented, 1872." These words in raised letters had happened to occupy just that part of the stove-hearth on which the child had seated herself, and being heated nearly to red heat they had reproduced themselves on the surface of the unfortunate child.

The law student entered into the mother's sorrow with much sympathy, but after he had in some degree calmed her mind he informed her that a breach of law had been committed. "Your child," he remarked, "has never been patented, but she is marked 'Patented, 1872.' This is an infringement of the statute. You falsely represent by that brand that a child for whom no patent was issued is patented. This false representation is forgery, and subjects you to penalty made and provided for that crime."

Mrs. Smith was, as may be supposed, greatly alarmed at learning this statement, and her first impulse was to beg the young man to save her from a convict's cell. With a gravity suited to the occasion, he explained the whole law of patents. He told her that had she desired to patent the child, she should have either constructed a model of it or prepared accurate drawings, with specifications showing distinctly what parts of the child she claimed to have invented. This model or these drawings she should have forwarded to the Patent Office, and she would then have received in due time a patent—provided, of course, the child was really patentable—and would have been authorised to label it "Patented." "Unfortunately," he pursued, "It is now too late to take this course, and we must boldly claim that a patent was issued, but that the record was destroyed during the recent fire in the Patent Office."

This suggestion cheered the spirits of Mrs. Smith, but they were again dashed by the further remarks of the young man. He reminded her that the child might find it very inconvenient to be patented. "If we claim," he went on to say, "that she has been regularly patented, it follows that the ownership of the patent, including the child herself, belongs to you, and will pass at your death into the possession of your heirs. Holding the patent, they can prevent any husband taki g possession of the girl by marriage, and they can sell, assign, transfer, and set over the patent right and the accompanying girl to any purchaser. If she is sold to a speculator or to a joint-stock company, she will find her position a most unpleasant one; patented or she is not. If she is not patented, you are guilty of forgery. If she is patented, she is an object of barter and sale, or in other words a chattel."

This was certainly a wretched state of things, and Mrs. Smith, to ease her mind, began to abuse Mrs. Brown, whose stove had branded the unfortunate little girl. She loudly insisted that the whole fault rested with Mrs. Brown, and demanded to know if the latter could not be punished. The young man, who was immensely learned in the law, thereupon began a new argument. He told her that where there is a wrong there must, in the nature of things, be a remedy. "Mrs. Brown, by means of her stove, has done you a great wrong. In accordance with the maxim, *Qui facit per alium facit per se*, Mrs. Brown, and not the stove, is the party from whom you must demand redress. She has wickedly and maliciously, and at the instigation of the devil, branded your child, and thus rendered you liable for an infringement of the patent law. It is my opinion, madam, that an action for assault and an action for libel will both lie against Mrs. Brown, and 'semble' that there is also ground for having her indicted for procurement of forgery." Finally, after much further argument, the young man advised her to apply to a magistrate and procure the arrest and punishment of Mrs. Brown.

Accordingly, Mrs. Smith applied to the Mayor, who, after vainly trying to comprehend the case, and to find out what was the precise crime alleged against Mrs. Brown, compromised the matter by unofficially asking the lady to appear before him. When both the ladies were in court Mrs. Smith prompted by the clerk, put her complaint in the shape of a charge that Mrs. Brown had branded the youthful Smith girl. The latter was then marked "Exhibit A," and formally put in evidence, and both complainant and defendant told their respective stories.

The result was that the court, in a very able and voluminous opinion, decided that nobody was guilty of anything, but that, with a view of avoiding the penalty of infringing the patent law, the mother must apply to Congress for a special act declaring the child regularly and legally patented.

If Congress finds time to attend to this important matter, little Miss Smith will be the first girl ever patented in this country, and the legal profession will watch with unflagging interest the lawsuits to which in future any infringement of the patent may lead.

Zenobia's Infidelity

H. C. Bunner

Dr. Tibbitt stood on the porch of Mrs. Pennypepper's boardinghouse, and looked up and down the deserted Main Street of Sagawaug with a contented smile, the while he buttoned his driving-gloves. The little doctor had good cause to be content with himself and with everything else—with his growing practice, with his comfortable boardinghouse, with his own good looks, with his neat attire, and with the world in general. He could not but be content with Sagawaug, for there never was a prettier country town. The Doctor looked across the street and picked out the very house that he proposed to buy when the one remaining desire of his soul was gratified. It was a house with a hip-roof and with a long garden running down to the river.

There was no one in the house today, but there was no one in any of the houses. Not even a pair of round bare arms was visible among the clothes that waved in the August breeze in every back-yard. It was Circus Day in Sagawaug.

The Doctor was climbing into his gig when a yell startled him. A freckled boy with saucer eyes dashed around the corner.

"Doctor!" he gasped, "come quick! The circus got a-fire an' the trick elephant's most roasted!"

"Don't be silly, Johnny," said the Doctor, reprovingly.

"Hope to die—Honest Injun—cross my breast!" said the boy. The Doctor knew the sacredness of this juvenile oath.

"Get in here with me," he said, "and if I find you're trying to be funny, I'll drop you in the river."

As they drove toward the outskirts of the town, Johnny told his tale.

"Now," he began, "the folks was all out of the tent after the show was over, and one of the circus men, he went to the oil-barrel in the green wagon with Dan'l in the Lion's Den onto the outside of it, an' he took in a candle an' left it there, and fust thing the barrel busted, an' he wasn't hurted a bit, but the trick elephant she was burned awful, an' the ring-tailed baboon, he was so scared he had a fit. Say, did you know baboons had fits?"

When they reached the circus-grounds, they found a crowd around a small side-show tent. A strong odor of burnt leather confirmed Johnny's story. Dr. Tibbitt pushed his way through the throng, and gazed upon the huge beast, lying on her side on the grass, her broad shoulder charred and quivering. Her bulk expanded and contracted with spasms of agony, and from time to time she uttered a moaning sound. On her head was a structure of red cloth, about the size of a bushel-basket, apparently intended to look like a British soldier's forage-cap. This was secured by a strap that went under her chin—if an elephant has a chin. The scarlet cheesebox every now and then slipped down over her eye and the faithful animal patiently, in all her anguish, adjusted it with her prehensile trunk.

By her side stood her keeper and the proprietor of the show, a large man with a dyed moustache, a wrinkled face, and hair oiled and frizzed. These two bewailed their loss alternately.

"The boss elephant in the business!" cried the showman. "Barnum never had no trick elephant like Zenobia. And them lynes and Dan'l was painted in new before I took the road this season. Oh, there's been a hoodoo on me since I showed ag'inst the Sunday-school picnic!"

"That there elephant's been like my own child," groaned the keeper, "or my own wife, I may say. I've slep' alongside of her every night for fourteen damn years."

The Doctor had been carefully examining his patient.

"If there is any analogy—" he began.

"Neuralogy!" snorted the indignant showman; " 'taint neuralogy, you jay pill-box, she's *cooked!*"

"If there is any analogy," repeated Dr. Tibbitt, flushing a little, "between her case and that of a human being, I think I can save your elephant. Get me a barrel of linseed oil, and drive these people away."

The Doctor's orders were obeyed with eager submission. He took off his coat, and went to work. He had never doctored an elephant, and the job interested him. At the end of an hour, Zenobia's sufferings were somewhat alleviated. She lay on her side, chained tightly to the ground, and swaddled in bandages. Her groans had ceased.

"I'll call to-morrow at noon," said the Doctor—"good gracious, what's that?" Zenobia's trunk was playing about his waistband.

"She wants to shake hands with you," her keeper explained. "She's a lady, she is, and she knows you done her good."

"I'd rather not have anything of the sort," said the Doctor, decisively.

When Dr. Tibbitt called at twelve on the morrow, he found Zenobia's tent neatly roped in, an amphitheatre of circus-benches constructed around her, and this amphitheatre packed with people.

"Got a quarter apiece from them jays," whispered the showman "jest to see you dress them wounds." Subsequently the showman relieved his mind to a casual acquaintance. "He's got a heart like a gun-flint, that doctor," he said; "made me turn out every one of them jays and give 'em their money back before he'd lay a hand to Zenobia."

But if the Doctor suppressed the clinic, neither he nor the showman suffered. From dawn till dusk people came from miles around to stare a quarter's worth at the burnt elephant. Once in a while, as a rare treat, the keeper lifted a corner of her bandages, and revealed the seared flesh. The show went off in a day or two, leaving Zenobia to recover at leisure; and as it wandered westward, it did an increased business simply because it had had a burnt trick elephant. Such, dear friends, is the human mind.

The Doctor fared even better. The fame of his new case spread far and wide. People seemed to think that if he could cure an elephant he could cure anything. He was called into consultation in neighboring towns. Women in robust health imagined ailments, so as to send for him and ask him shuddering questions about "that *wretched* animal." The trustees of the orphan-asylum made him staff-physician—in this case the Doctor thought he could trade a connection of ideas, in which children and circus were naturally associated. And the local newspaper called him a *savant*.

He called every day upon Zenobia, who greeted him with trumpetings of joyful welcome. She also desired to shake hands with him, and her keeper had to sit on her head and hold her trunk to repress the familiarity. In two weeks she was cured, except for extensive and permanent scars, and she waited only for a favorable opportunity to rejoin the circus.

The Doctor had got his fee in advance.

Upon a sunny afternoon in the last of August, Dr. Tibbitt jogged slowly toward Sagawaug in his neat little gig. He had been to Pelion, the next town, to call upon Miss Minetta Bunker, the young lady whom he desired to install in the house with the garden running down to the river. He had found her starting out for a drive in Tom Matson's dog-cart. Now, the Doctor feared no foe, in medicine or in love; but when a young woman is inscrutable as to the state of her affections, when the richest young man in the county is devoting himself to her, and when the young lady's mother is backing the rich man, a young country doctor may well feel perplexed and anxious over his chance of the prize.

The Doctor was so troubled, indeed, that he paid no heed to a heavy, repeated thud behind him, on the macadamized road. His gentle little mare heard it, though, and began to curvet and prance. The Doctor

was pulling her in, and calming her with a "Soo—
Soo—down, girl, down!" when he interrupted himself
to shout:

"Great Caesar! get off me!"

Something like a yard of rubber hose had come in
through the side of the buggy, and was rubbing itself
against his face. He looked around, and the cold sweat
stood out on him as he saw Zenobia, her chain dragging from her hind-foot, her red cap a-cock on her
head, trotting along by the side of his vehicle, snorting
with joy, and evidently bent on lavishing her pliant,
serpentine, but leathery caresses upon his person.

His fear vanished in a moment. The animal's intentions were certainly pacific, to put it mildly. He reflected that if he could keep his horse ahead of her, he
could toll her around the block and back toward her
tent. He had hardly guessed, as yet, the depth of the
impression which he had made upon Zenobia's heart,
which must have been a large organ, if the size of her
ears was an indication—according to the popular
theory.

He was on the very edge of the town, and his road
took him by a house where he had a new and highly
valued patient, the young wife of old Deacon Burgee.
Her malady being of a nature that permitted it, Mrs.
Burgee was in the habit of sitting at her window when
the Doctor made his rounds, and indicating the satis-
factory state of her health by a bow and a smile. On
this occasion she fled from the window with a shriek.
Her mother, a formidable old lady under a red false-
front, came to the window, shrieked likewise, and
slammed down the sash.

The Doctor tolled his elephant around the block

without further misadventure, and they started up the road toward Zenobia's tent, Zenobia caressing her benefactor while shudders of antipathy ran over his frame. In a few minutes the keeper hove in sight. Zenobia saw him first, blew a shrill blast on her trumpet, close to the Doctor's ear, bolted through a snake-fence, lumbered across a turnipfield, and disappeared in a patch of woods, leaving the Doctor to quiet his excited horse and to face the keeper who advanced with rage in his eye.

"What do you mean, you cuss," he began, "weaning a man's elephant's affections away from him? You ain't got no more morals than a Turk, you ain't. That elephant an' me has been side-partners for fourteen years, an' here you come between us."

"I don't want your confounded elephant," roared the Doctor, "why don't you keep it chained up?"

"She busted her chain to git after you," replied the keeper. "Oh, I seen you two lally-gaggin' all along the road. I knowed you wa'n't no good the first time I set eyes on yer, a-sayin' hoodoo words over the poor dumb beast."

The Doctor resolved to banish "analogy" from his vocabulary.

The next morning, about four o'clock, Dr. Tibbitt awoke with a troubled mind. He had driven home after midnight from a late call, and he had had an uneasy fancy that he saw a great shadowy bulk ambling along in the mist-hid fields by the roadside. He jumped out of bed and went to the window. Below him, completely covering Mrs. Pennypepper's nasturtium bed, her prehensile trunk ravaging the early chrysanthemums, stood Zenobia, swaying to and fro, the dew glistening on her seamed sides beneath the early morning sunlight. The Doctor hastily dressed himself and slipped downstairs and out, to meet this Frankenstein's monster of affection.

There was but one thing to do. Zenobia would follow him wherever he went—she rushed madly through Mrs. Pennypepper's roses to greet him—and his only course was to lead her out of the town before people began to get up, and to detain her in some remote meadow until he could get her keeper to come for her and secure her by force or stratagem. He set off by the least frequented streets, and he experienced a pang of horror as he remembered that his way led him past the house of his one professional rival in Sagawaug. Suppose Dr. Pettengill should be coming home or going out as he passed!

He did not meet Dr. Pettengill. He did meet Deacon Burgee, who stared at him with more of rage than of amazement in his wrinkled countenance. The Deacon was carrying a large bundle of embroidered linen and flannel, that must have been tied up in a hurry.

"Good morning, Deacon," the Doctor hailed him, with as much ease of manner as he could assume. "How's Mrs. Burgee?"

"She's doin' fust rate, no thanks to no circus doctors!" snorted the Deacon. "An' if you want to know anything further concernin' her health, you ask Dr. Pettengill. *He's* got more sense than to go trailin' around the streets with a parboiled elephant behind him, a-frightening women-folks a hull month afore th'r time."

"Why, Deacon!" cried the Doctor, "what—what is it?"

"It's a boy, responded the Deacon sternly; "and it's God's own mercy that 'twa'nt born with a trunk and a tail."

The Doctor found a secluded pasture near the woods that encircled the town, and there he sat him down, in the corner of a snake-fence, to wait until some farmer or market-gardener should pass by, to carry his message to the keeper. He had another message to send, too. He had several cases that must be attended to at once. Unless he could get away from his pachydermatous familiar, Pettengill must care for his cases that morning. It was hard—but what was he to do?

Zenobia stood by his side, dividing her attention between the caresses she bestowed on him and the care she was obliged to take of her red cap, which was not tightly strapped on, and slipped in various directions at every movement of her gigantic head. She was unmistakably happy. From time to time she trumpeted cheerily. She plucked up tufts of grass, and offered them to the Doctor. He refused them, and she ate them herself. Once he took a daisy from her, absent-mindedly, and she was so greatly pleased that she smashed his hat in her endeavors to pet him. The Doctor was a kind-hearted man. He had to admit that Zenobia meant well. He patted her trunk, and made matters worse. Her elephantine ecstasy came near being the death of him.

Still the farmer came not, nor the market-gardener. Dr. Tibbitt began to believe that he had chosen a meadow that was *too* secluded. At last two boys appeared. After they had stared at him and at Zenobia for half an hour, one of them agreed to produce Dr. Pettengill and Zenobia's keeper for fifty cents. Dr. Pettengill was the first to arrive. He refused to come nearer than the furthest limit of the pasture.

"Hello, Doctor," he called out, "hear you've been seeing elephants. Want me to take your cases? Guess I can. Got a half-hour free. Brought some bromide down for you, if you'd like to try it."

To judge from his face, Zenobia was invisible. But his presence alarmed that sensitive animal. She crowded up close to the fence, and every time she flicked her skin to shake off the flies she endangered the equilibrium of the Doctor, who was sitting on the top rail, for dignity's sake. He shouted his directions to his colleague, who shouted back professional criticisms.

"Salicylate of soda for that old woman? What's the matter with salicylate of cinchonidia? Don't want to kill her before you get out of this swamp, do you?"

Dr. Tibbitt was not a profane man; but at this moment he could not restrain himself.

"*Damn you!*" he said, with such vigor that the elephant gave a convulsive start. The Doctor felt his seat depart from under him—he was going—going into space for a brief moment, and then he scrambled up out of the soft mud of the cow-wallow back of the fence on which he had been sitting. Zenobia had backed against the fence.

The keeper arrived soon after. He had only reached the meadow when Zenobia lifted her trunk in the air, emitted a mirthful toot, and struck out for the woods with the picturesque and cumbersome gallop of a mastodon pup.

"Dern *you*," said the keeper to Dr. Tibbitt, who was trying to fasten his collar, which had broken loose in his fall; "if the boys was here, and I hollered 'Hey Rube!'—there wouldn't be enough left of yer to spread a plaster for a baby's bile!"

The Doctor made himself look as decent as the situation allowed, and then he marched toward the town with the light of a firm resolve illuminating his face. The literature of his childhood had come to his aid. He remembered the unkind tailor who pricked the elephant's trunk. It seemed to him that the tailor was a rather good fellow.

"If that elephant's disease is gratitude," thought the Doctor, "I'll give her an antidote."

He went to the drug-store, and as he went, he pulled out a blank pad and wrote down a prescription, from mere force of habit. It read thus:

PESSELS & MORTON,
Druggists,
Commercial Block, Main Street,
Sagawaug
Prescriptions carefully compounded
RX Calcium sul Zij
Calcis chl $z \times 2j$
Capricam pulv Zi
Mi et ft. Bol.
Sig Take at once
Tibbitt

When the druggist looked at it, he was taken short of breath.

"What's this?" he asked—"a bombshell?"

"Put it up," said the Doctor, "and don't talk so much." He lingered nervously on the druggist's steps, looking up and down the street. He had sent a boy to order the stable-man to harness his gig. By-and-by, the druggist put his head out of the door.

"I've got some asafoetida pills," he said, "that are kind o' tired, and half a pound of whale-oil soap that's higher 'n Haman—"

"Put 'em in!" said the Doctor, grimly; as he saw Zenobia coming in sight far down the street.

She came up while the Doctor was waiting for the bolus. Twenty-three boys were watching them, although it was only seven o'clock in the morning.

"Down, Zenobia!" said the Doctor, thoughtlessly, as he might have addressed a dog. He was talking with the druggist, and Zenobia was patting his ear with her trunk. Zenobia sank to her knees. The Doctor did not notice her. She folded her trunk about him, lifted him to her back, rose, with a heave and a sway, to her feet, and started up the road. The boys cheered. The Doctor got off on the end of an elm-branch. His descent was watched from nineteen second-story windows.

His gig came to meet him at last, and he entered it and drove rapidly out of town, with Zenobia trotting contentedly behind him. As soon as he had passed Deacon Burgee's house, he drew rein, and Zenobia approached, while his perspiring mare stood on her hind legs.

"Zenobia—pill!" said the Doctor.

As she had often done in her late illness, Zenobia opened her mouth at the word of command, and swallowed the infernal bolus. Then they started up again, and the Doctor headed for Zenobia's tent.

But Zenobia's pace was sluggish. She had been

dodging about woods for two nights, and she was tired. When the Doctor whipped up, she seized the buggy by any convenient projection, and held it back. This damaged the buggy and frightened the horse; but it accomplished Zenobia's end. It was eleven o'clock before Jake Bumgardner's "Half-Way House" loomed up white, afar down the dusty road, and the Doctor knew that his round-about way had at length brought him near to the field where the circus-tent had been pitched.

He drove on with a lighter heart in his bosom. He had not heard Zenobia behind him for some time. He did not know what had become of her, or what she was doing, but he learned later.

The Doctor had compounded a pill well calculated to upset Zenobia's stomach. That it would likewise give her a consuming thirst he had not considered. But chemistry was doing its duty without regard to him. A thirst like a furnace burned within Zenobia. Capsicum and chloride of lime were doing their work. She gasped and groaned. She searched for water. She filled her trunk at a wayside trough and poured the contents into her mouth. Then she sucked up a puddle or two. Then she came to Bumgardner's, where a dozen kegs of lager-beer and a keg of what passed at Bumgardner's for gin stood on the sidewalk. Zenobia's circus experience had taught her what a water-barrel meant. She applied her knowledge. With her forefoot she deftly staved in the head of one keg after another, and with her trunk she drew up the beer and the gin, and delivered them to her stomach. If you think her taste at fault, remember the bolus.

Bumgardner rushed out and assailed her with a

bung-starter. She turned upon him and squirted lager-beer over him until he was covered with an iridescent lather of foam from head to foot. Then she finished the kegs and went on her way, to overtake the Doctor.

The Doctor was speeding his mare merrily along, grateful for even a momentary relief from Zenobia's attentions, when, at one and the same time, he heard a heavy, uncertain thumping on the road behind him, and the quick patter of a trotter's hoofs on the road ahead of him. He glanced behind him first, and saw Zenobia. She swayed from side to side, more than was her wont. Her red cap was far down over her left eye. Her aspect was rakish, and her gait was unsteady. The Doctor did not know it, but Zenobia was drunk.

Zenobia was sick, but intoxication dominated her sickness. Even sulphide of calcium withdrew courteously before the might of beer and gin. Rocking from side to side, reeling across the road and back, trumpeting in imbecile inexpressive tones, Zenobia advanced.

The Doctor looked forward. Tom Matson sat in his dog-cart, with Miss Bunker by his side. His horse had caught sight of Zenobia and he was rearing high in air, and whinnying in terror. Before Tom could pull him down, he made a sudden break, overturned the dog-cart, and flung Tom and Miss Minetta Bunker on a bank by the side of the road. It was a soft bank, well-grown with mint and stinging-nettles, just above a creek. Tom had scarce landed before he was up and off, running hard across the fields.

Miss Minetta rose and looked at him with fire in her eyes.

"Well!" she said aloud; "I'd like Mother to see you *now!*"

The Doctor had jumped out of his gig and let his mare go galloping up the road. He had his arm about Miss Minetta's waist when he turned to face his familiar demon—which may have accounted for the pluck in his face.

But Zenobia was a hundred yards down the road, and she was utterly incapable of getting any further. She trumpeted once or twice, then she wavered like a reed in the wind; her legs weakened under her and she sank on her side. Her red cap had slipped down, and she picked it up with her trunk, broke its band in a reckless swing that resembled the wave of jovial farewell, gave one titanic hiccup, and fell asleep by the roadside.

An hour later, Dr. Tibbitt was driving toward Pelion, with Miss Bunker by his side. His horse had been stopped at the toll-gate. He was driving with one hand. Perhaps he needed the other to show how they could have a summer-house in the garden that ran down to the river.

But it was evening when Zenobia awoke to find her keeper sitting on her head. He jabbed a cotton-hook firmly and decisively into her ear, and led her homeward down the road lit by the golden sunset. That was the end of Zenobia's infidelity.

His Pa Plays Jokes

George Peck

"Say, do you think a little practical joke does any hurt?" asked the bad boy of the grocery man, as he came in with his Sunday suit on, and a bouquet in his buttonhole, and pried off a couple of figs from a new box that had been just opened.

"No sir," said the grocery man, as he licked off the syrup that dripped from a quart measure, from which he had been filling a jug. "I hold that a man who gets mad at a practical joke, that is, one that does not injure him, is a fool, and he ought to be shunned by all decent people. That's a nice bouquet you have in your coat. What is it, pansies? Let me smell of it," and the grocery man bent over in front of the boy to take a whiff at the bouquet. As he did so a stream of water shot out of the innocent looking bouquet and struck him full in the face, and run down over his shirt, and the grocery man yelled murder, and fell over a barrel of axe helves and scythe snaths, and then groped around for a towel to wipe his face.

"You condemn skunk," said the grocery man to the boy, as he took up an axe helve and started for him, "what kind of a golblasted squirt gun have you got there. I will maul you, by thunder," and he rolled up his shirt sleeves.

"There, keep your temper. I took a test vote of you on the subject of practical jokes, before the machine began to play upon the conflagration that was raging on your whiskey nose, and you said that a man who would get mad at a joke was a fool, and now I know it. Here let me show it to you. There is a rubber hose runs from the bouquet, inside my coat to my pants pocket, and there is a bulb of rubber, that holds about half a pint, and when a feller smells of the posey, I squeeze the bulb, and you see the result. It's fun, where you don't squirt it on a person that gets mad."

The grocery man said he would give the boy half a pound of figs if he would lend the bouquet to him for half an hour, to play it on a customer, and the boy fixed it on the grocery man, and turned the nozzle so it would squirt right back into the grocery man's face. He tried it on the first customer that came in, and got it right in his own face, and then the bulb in his pants pocket got to leaking, and the rest of the water ran down the grocery man's trousers' leg, and he gave it up in disgust, and handed it back to the boy.

"How was it your Pa had to be carried home from the sociable in a hack the other night?" asked the grocery man, as he stood close to the stove so his pants leg would dry. "He has not got to drinking again, has he?"

"O, no," said the boy, as he filled the bulb with vinegar, to practice on his chum. "It was this bouquet that got Pa into the trouble. You see I got Pa to smell of it, and I just filled him chuck full of water. He got mad and called me all kinds of names, and said I was no good on earth, and I would fetch up in state's prison, and then he wanted to borrow it to wear to the sociable. He said he would have more fun than you could shake a stick at, and I asked him if he didn't think he would fetch up in state's prison, and he said it was different with a man. He said when a man played a joke there was a certain dignity about it that was lacking in a boy. So I lent it to him, and we all went to the sociable in the basement of the church. I never see Pa more kitteny than he was that night. He filled the bulb with ice water, and the first one he got to smell of his button-hole bouquet was an old maid who thinks Pa is a heathen, but she likes to be made something of by anybody that wears pants, and when Pa sidled up to her and began talking about what a great work the christian wimmen of the land were doing in educating the heathen, she felt real good, and then she noticed Pa's posey in his button-hole and she touched it, and then she reached over her beak to smell of it. Pa he squeezed the bulb, and about half a teacupful of water struck her right in the nose, and some went into her strangle place, and *O, my*, didn't she yell. The sisters gathered around her and they said her face was all covered with perspiration and the paint was coming off, and they took her in the kitchen, and she told them Pa had slapped her with a dish of ice cream, and the wimmin told the minister and the deacons, and they went to Pa for an explanation, and Pa told them it was not so, and the minister got interested and got near Pa, and Pa let the water go at him, and hit him in the eye, and then a deacon got a dose, and Pa laughed; and then the minister who used to go to college, and be a hazer, and box, he got mad and squared off and hit Pa three times right by the eye, and one of the deacons kicked Pa, and Pa got mad and said he could clean out the whole shebang, and began to pull off his coat, when they bundled him out doors, and Ma got mad to see Pa abused, and she left the sociable, and I had to stay and eat ice cream and things for the whole family. Pa says that settles it with him. He says they haven't got any more christian charity in the church than they have in a tannery. His eyes are just getting over being black from the sparring lessons, and now he has got to go through oysters and beefsteak cure again. He says it is all owing to me."

"Well, what has all this got to do with your putting up signs in front of my store, 'Rotten Eggs,' and 'Frowy Butter a specialty,' " said the grocery man as he took the boy by the ear and pulled him around. "You have got an idea you are smart, and I want you to keep away from here. The next time I catch you in here I shall call the police and have you pulled. Now git!"

The boy pulled his ear back on the side of his head where it belonged, took out a cigarette and lit it, and after puffing smoke in the face of the grocery cat that was sleeping on the cover to the sugar barrel he said:

"If I was a provision pirate that never sold anything but what was spoiled so it couldn't be sold in a first-class store, who cheated in weights and measures, who bought only wormy figs and decayed cod-fish, who got his butter from a fat rendering establishment, his cider from a vinegar factory, and his sugar from a glucose factory, I would not insult the son of one of the finest families. Why, sir, I could go out on the corner, and when I saw customers coming here, I could tell a story that would turn their stomachs, and send them to the grocery on the next corner. Suppose I should tell them that the cat sleeps in the dried apple barrel, that the mice made nests in the prune box, and rats run riot through the raisins, and that you never wash your hands except on Decoration day and Christmas, that you wipe your nose on your shirt sleeves, and that you have the itch, do you think your business would be improved? Suppose I should tell customers that you buy sour kraut of a wooden-shoed Polacker, who makes it of pieces of cabbage that he gets by gathering swill, and sells that stuff to respectable people, could you pay your rent? If I should tell them that you put lozengers in the collection plate at church, and charge the minister forty cents a pound for oleomargarine, you would have to close up. Old man, I am onto you, and now you apologize for pulling my ear."

The grocery man turned pale during the recital, and finally said the bad boy was one of the best little fellows in this town, and the boy went out and hung up a sign in front: Girl wanted to cook.

The Ransom of Red Chief

O. Henry

It looked like a good thing; but wait till I tell you. We were down South, in Alabama—Bill Driscoll and myself—when this kidnapping idea struck us. It was, as Bill afterward expressed it, "during a moment of temporary mental apparition"; but we didn't find that out till later.

There was a town down there, as flat as flannel-cake, and called Summit, of course. It contained inhabitants of as undeleterious and self-satisfied a class of peasantry as ever clustered around a Maypole.

Bill and me had a joint capital of about $600, and we needed just $2000 more to pull off a fraudulent town-lot scheme in Western Illinois with. We talked it over on the front steps of the hotel. Philoprogenitiveness, says we, is strong in semirural communities; therefore, and for other reasons, a kidnapping project ought to do better there than in the radius of newspapers that send reporters out in plain clothes to stir up talk about such things. We knew that Summit couldn't get after us with anything stronger than constables, and, maybe, some lackadaisical bloodhounds and a diatribe or two in the *Weekly Farmers' Budget*. So it looked good.

We selected for our victim the only child of a prominent citizen named Ebenezer Dorset. The father was respectable and tight, a mortgage fancier and a stern, upright collection-plate passer and forecloser. The kid was a boy of ten, with bas-relief freckles, and hair the color of the cover of the magazine you buy at the newsstand when you want to catch a train. Bill and me figured that Ebenezer would melt down for a ransom of $2000 to a cent. But wait till I tell you.

About two miles from Summit was a little mountain, covered with a dense cedar brake. On the rear elevation of this mountain was a cave. There we stored provisions.

One evening after sundown we drove in a buggy past old Dorset's house. The kid was in the street, throwing rocks at a kitten on the opposite fence.

"Hey, little boy!" says Bill, "would you like to have a bag of candy and a nice ride?"

The boy catches Bill neatly in the eye with a piece of brick.

"That will cost the old man an extra five hundred dollars," says Bill, climbing over the wheel.

That boy put up a fight like a welterweight cinnamon bear; but at last we got him down in the bottom of the buggy and drove away. We took him up to the cave, and I hitched the horse in the cedar brake. After dark I drove the buggy to the little village, three miles away, where we had hired it, and walked back to the mountain.

Bill was pasting court plaster over the scratches and bruises on his features. There was a fire burning behind the big rock at the entrance of the cave, and the boy was watching a pot of boiling coffee, with two buzzard-tail feathers stuck in his red hair. He points a stick at me when I come up, and says:

"Ha! Cursed paleface, do you dare to enter the camp of Red Chief, the terror of the plains?"

"He's all right now," says Bill, rolling up his trousers and examining some bruises on his shins. "We're playing Indian. We're making Buffalo Bill's show look like magic-lantern views of Palestine in the town hall. I'm Old Hank, the Trapper, Red Chief's captive, and I'm to be scalped at daybreak. By Geronimo! That kid can kick hard."

Yes, sir, that boy seemed to be having the time of his life. The fun of camping out in a cave made him forget that he was a captive himself. He immediately christened me Snake-eye the Spy, and announced that, when his braves returned from the warpath, I was to be broiled at the stake at the rising of the sun.

Then we had supper, and he filled his mouth full of bacon and bread and gravy, and began to talk. He made a during-dinner speech something like this:

"I like this fine. I never camped out before; but I had a pet 'possum once, and I was nine last birthday. I hate to go to school. Rats ate up sixteen of Jimmy Talbot's aunt's speckled hen's eggs. Are there any real Indians in these woods? I want some more gravy. Does the trees moving make the wind blow? We had five puppies. What makes your nose so red Hank? My father has lots of money. Are the stars hot? I whipped Ed Walker twice, Saturday. I don't like girls. You dassent catch toads unless with a string. Do oxen make any noise? Why are oranges round? Have you got beds to sleep on in this cave? Amos Murray has got six toes.

A parrot can talk, but a monkey or a fish can't. How many does it take to make twelve?"

Every few minutes he would remember that he was a pesky redskin, and pick up his stick rifle and tiptoe to the mouth of the cave to rubber for the scouts of the hated paleface. Now and then he would let out a war whoop that made Old Hank the Trapper shiver. The boy had Bill terrorized from the start.

"Red Chief," says I to the kid, "would you like to go home?"

"Aw, what for?" says he. "I don't have any fun at home. I hate to go to school. I like to camp out. You won't take me back home again, Snake-eye, will you?"

"Not right away," says I. "We'll stay here in the cave a while."

"All right!" says he. "That'll be fine. I never had such fun in all my life."

We went to bed about 11 o'clock. We spread down some wide blankets and quilts and put Red Chief between us. We weren't afraid he'd run away. He kept us awake for three hours, humping up and reaching for his rifle and screeching: "Hist! pard," in mine and Bill's ears, as the fancied crackle of a twig or the rustle of a leaf revealed to his young imagination the stealthy approach of the outlaw band. At last, I fell into a troubled sleep, and dreamed that I had been kidnapped and chained to a tree by a ferocious pirate with red hair.

Just at daybreak I was awakened by a series of awful screams from Bill. They weren't yells, or howls, or shouts, or whoops, or yawps, such as you'd expect from a manly set of vocal organs—they were simply indecent, terrifying, humiliating screams, such as women emit when they see ghosts or caterpillars. It's an awful thing to hear a strong, desperate, fat man scream incontinently in a cave at daybreak.

I jumped up to see what the matter was. Red Chief was sitting on Bill's chest, with one hand twined in Bill's hair. In the other he had the sharp case knife we used for slicing bacon; and he was industriously and realistically trying to take Bill's scalp, according to the sentence that had been pronounced upon him the evening before.

I got the knife away from the kid and made him lie down again. But from that moment Bill's spirit was broken. He laid down on his side of the bed, but he never closed an eye again in sleep as long as that boy was with us. I dozed for a while, but along toward sunup I remembered that Red Chief had said I was to be burned at the stake at the rising of the sun. I wasn't nervous or afraid, but I sat up and lit my pipe and leaned against a rock.

"What you getting up so soon for, Sam?" asked Bill.

"Me?" says I. "Oh, I got a kind of a pain in my shoulder. I thought sitting up would rest it."

"You're a liar!" says Bill. "You're afraid. You was to be burned at sunrise, and you was afraid he'd do it. And he would, too, if he could find a match. Ain't it awful, Sam? Do you think anybody will pay out money to get a little imp like that back home?"

"Sure," said I. "A rowdy kid like that is just the kind that parents dote on. Now, you and the Chief get up and cook breakfast, while I go up on the top of this mountain and reconnoiter."

I went up on the peak of the little mountain and ran my eye over the contiguous vicinity. Over toward

Summit I expected to see the sturdy yeomanry of the village armed with scythes and pitchforks beating the countryside for the dastardly kidnappers. But what I saw was a peaceful landscape dotted with one man ploughing with a dun mule. Nobody was dragging the creek; no couriers dashed hither and yon, bringing tidings of no news to the distracted parents. There was a sylvan attitude of somnolent sleepiness pervading that section of the external outward surface of Alabama that lay exposed to my view. "Perhaps," says I to myself, "it has not yet been discovered that the wolves have borne away the tender lambkin from the fold. Heaven help the wolves!" says I, and went down the mountain to breakfast.

When I got to the cave I found Bill backed up against the side of it, breathing hard, and the boy threatening to smash him with a rock half as big as a coconut.

"He put a red-hot boiled potato down my back," explained Bill, "and then mashed it with his foot; and I boxed his ears. Have you got a gun about you, Sam?"

I took the rock away from the boy and kind of patched up the argument. "I'll fix you," says the kid to Bill. "No man ever yet struck the Red Chief but what he got paid for it. You better beware!"

After breakfast the kid takes a piece of leather with strings wrapped around it out of his pocket and goes outside the cave unwinding it.

"What's he up to now?" says Bill anxiously. "You don't think he'll run away, do you, Sam?"

"No fear of it," says I. "He don't seem to be much of a homebody. But we've got to fix up some plan about the ransom. There don't seem to be much excitement around Summit on account of his disappearance; but maybe they think he's spending the night with Aunt Jane or one of the neighbors. Anyhow, he'll be missed today. Tonight we must get a message to his father demanding the two thousand dollars for his return."

Just then we heard a kind of war whoop, such as David might have emitted when he knocked out the champion Goliath. It was a sling that Red Chief had pulled out of his pocket, and he was whirling it around his head.

I dodged, and heard a heavy thud and a kind of a sigh from Bill, like a horse gives out when you take his saddle off. A rock the size of an egg had caught Bill just behind his left ear. He loosened himself all over and fell in the fire across the frying pan of hot water for washing the dishes. I dragged him out and poured cold water on his head for half an hour.

By and by, Bill sits up and feels behind his ear and says: "Sam, do you know who my favorite Biblical character is?"

"Take it easy," says I. "You'll come to your senses presently."

"King Herod," says he. "You won't go away and leave me here alone, will you, Sam?"

I went out and caught that boy and shook him until his freckles rattled.

"If you don't behave," says, I, "I'll take you straight home. Now, are you going to be good, or not?"

"I was only funning," says he sullenly. "I didn't mean to hurt Old Hank. But what did he hit me for? I'll behave, Snake-eye, if you won't send me home, and if you'll let me play the Black Scout today."

"I don't know the game," says I. "That's for you and

Mr. Bill to decide. He's your playmate for the day. I'm going away for a while, on business. Now, you come in and make friends with him and say you are sorry for hurting him, or home you go, at once."

I made him and Bill shake hands, and then I took Bill aside and told him I was going to Poplar Cove, a little village three miles from the cave, and find out what I could about how the kidnapping had been regarded in Summit. Also, I thought it best to send a preemptory letter to old man Dorset that day, demanding the ransom and dictating how it should be paid.

"You know, Sam," says Bill, "I've stood by you without batting an eye in earthquakes, fire, and flood—in poker games, dynamite outrages, police raids, train robberies, and cyclones. I never lost my nerve yet till we kidnapped that two-legged skyrocket of a kid. He's got me going. You won't leave me long with him, will you, Sam?"

"I'll be back sometime this afternoon," says I. "You must keep the boy amused and quiet till I return. And now we'll write the letter to old Dorsey."

Bill and I got paper and pencil and worked on the letter while Red Chief, with a blanket wrapped around him, strutted up and down, guarding the mouth of the cave. Bill begged me tearfully to make the ransom $1500 instead of $2000. "I ain't attempting," says he, "to decry the celebrated moral aspect of parental affection, but we're dealing with humans, and it ain't human for anybody to give up two thousand dollars for that forty-pound chunk of freckled wildcat. I'm willing to take a chance at fifteen hundred dollars. You can charge the difference up to me."

So, to relieve Bill, I acceded, and we collaborated a letter that ran this way:

Ebenezer Dorset, Esq.:

We have your boy concealed in a place far from Summit. It is useless for you or the most skilled detectives to attempt to find him. Absolutely the only terms on which you can have him restored to you are these: We demand $1500 in large bills for his return: the money to be left at midnight at the same spot and in the same box as your reply—as hereinafter described. If you agree to these terms, send your answer in writing by a solitary messenger tonight at half-past eight o'clock. After crossing Owl Creek, on the road to Poplar Cove, there are three large trees about a hundred yards apart, close to the fence of the wheat field on the right-hand side. At the bottom of the fence post opposite the third tree will be found a small pasteboard box.

The messenger will place the answer in this box and return immediately to Summit.

If you attempt any treachery or fail to comply with our demand as stated, you will never see your boy again.

If you pay the money as demanded, he will be returned to you safe and well within three hours. These terms are final, and if you do not accede to them no further communication will be attempted.

Two Desperate Men

I addressed this letter to Dorset, and put it in my pocket. As I was about to start, the kid comes up to me and says:

"Aw, Snake-eye, you said I could play the Black Scout while you was gone."

"Play it, of course," says I. "Mr. Bill will play with you. What kind of a game is it?"

"I'm the Black Scout," says the Red Chief, "and I have to ride to the stockade to warn the settlers that the Indians are coming. I'm tired of playing Indian myself. I want to be the Black Scout."

"All right," says I. "It sounds harmless to me. I guess Mr. Bill will help you foil the pesky savages."

"What am I to do?" asks Bill, looking at the kid suspiciously.

"You are the hoss," says Black Scout. "Get down on your hands and knees. How can I ride to the stockade without a hoss?"

"You'd better keep him interested," said I, "till we get the scheme going. Loosen up."

Bill gets down on his all fours, and a look comes in his eye like a rabbit's when you catch it in a trap.

"How far is it to the stockade, kid?" he asks, in a husky manner of voice.

"Ninety miles," says the Black Scout. "And you have to hump yourself to get there on time. Whoa, now!"

The Black Scout jumps on Bill's back and digs his heels in his side.

"For heaven's sake," says Bill, "hurry back, Sam, as soon as you can. I wish we hadn't made the ransom more than a thousand. Say, you quit kicking me or I'll get up and warm you good."

I walked over to Poplar Cove and sat around the post office and store, talking with the chawbacons that came in to trade. One whiskerando says that he hears Summit is all upset on account of Elder Ebenezer Dorset's boy having been lost or stolen. That was all I wanted to know. I bought some smoking tobacco, referred casually to the price of blackeyed peas, posted my letter surreptitiously and came away. The postmaster said the mail carrier would come by in an hour to take the mail on to Summit.

When I got back to the cave Bill and the boy were not to be found. I explored the vicinity of the cave, and risked a yodel or two, but there was no response.

So I lighted my pipe and sat down on a mossy bank to await developments.

In about half an hour I heard the bushes rustle, and Bill wobbled out into the little glade in front of the cave. Behind him was the kid, stepping softly like a scout, with a broad grin on his face. Bill stopped, took off his hat and wiped his face with a red handkerchief. The kid stopped about eight feet behind him.

"Sam," says Bill, "I suppose you think I'm a renegade, but I couldn't help it. I'm a grown person with masculine proclivities and habits of self-defense, but there is a time when all systems of egotism and predominance fail. The boy is gone. I have sent him home. All is off. There was martyrs in old times," goes on Bill, "that suffered death rather than give up the particular graft they enjoyed. None of 'em was subjugated to such supernatural tortures as I have been. I tried to be faithful to our articles of depredation; but there came a limit."

"What's the trouble, Bill?" I asks him.

"I was rode," says Bill, "the ninety miles to the stockade, not barring an inch. Then, when the settlers was rescued, I was given oats. Sand ain't a palatable substitute. And then, for an hour I had to try to explain to him why there was nothin' in holes, how a road can run both ways and what makes the grass green. I tell you, Sam, a human can only stand so much. I takes him by the neck of his clothes and drags him down the mountain. On the way he kicks my legs black-and-blue from the knees down; and I've got to have two or three bites on my thumb and hand cauterized.

"But he's gone—" continues Bill—"gone home. I showed him the road to Summit and kicked him about eight feet nearer there at one kick. I'm sorry we lose the ransom; but it was either that or Bill Driscoll to the madhouse."

Bill is puffing and blowing, but there is a look of ineffable peace and growing content on his rose-pink features.

"Bill," says I, "there isn't any heart disease in your family, is there?"

"No," says Bill, "nothing chronic except malaria and accidents. Why?"

"Then you might turn around," says I, "and have a look behind you."

Bill turns and sees the boy, and loses his complexion and sits down plump on the ground and begins to pluck aimlessly at grass and little sticks. For an hour I was afraid of his mind. And then I told him that my scheme was to put the whole job through immediately and that we would get the ransom and be off with it by midnight if old Dorset fell in with our proposition. So Bill braced up enough to give the kid a weak sort of smile and a promise to play the Russian in a Japanese war with him as soon as he felt a little better.

I had a scheme for collecting that ransom without danger of being caught by counterplots that ought to commend itself to professional kidnappers. The tree under which the answer was to be left—and the money

later on—was close to the road fence with big, bare
fields on all sides. If a gang of constables should be
watching for anyone to come for the note they could
see him a long way off crossing the fields or in the
road. But no, siree! At half past eight I was up in that
tree as well hidden as a tree toad, waiting for the
messenger to arrive.

Exactly on time, a half-grown boy rides up the road
on a bicycle, locates the pasteboard box at the foot of
the fence post, slips a folded piece of paper into it and
pedals away again back toward Summit.

I waited an hour and then concluded the thing was
square. I slid down the tree, got the note, slipped
along the fence till I struck the woods, and was back at
the cave in another half an hour. I opened the note, got
near the lantern and read it to Bill. It was written with
a pen in a crabbed hand, and the sum and substance of
it was this:

Two Desperate Men
 Gentlemen: I received your letter today by post, in regard to
the ransom you asked for the return of my son. I think you are a
little high in your demands, and I hereby make you a counter-
proposition, which I am inclined to believe you will accept. You
bring Johnny home and pay me $250 in cash, and I agree to take
him off your hands. You had better come at night, for the neighbors believe he is lost, and I couldn't be responsible for what they
would do to anybody they saw bringing him back.
 Very respectfully,
 Ebenezer Dorset

"Great pirates of Penzance!" says I. "Of all the
impudent—"

But I glanced at Bill, and hesitated. He had the

most appealing look in his eyes I ever saw on the face of a dumb or talking brute.

"Sam," says he, "what's two hundred and fifty dollars, after all? We've got the money. One more night of this kid will send me to bed in Bedlam. Besides being a thorough gentleman, I think Mr. Dorset is a spendthrift for making us such a liberal offer. You ain't going to let the chance go, are you?"

"Tell you the truth, Bill," says I, "this little he ewe lamb has somewhat got on my nerves, too. We'll take him home, pay the ransom, and make our getaway."

We took him home that night. We got him to go by telling him that his father had bought a silver-mounted rifle and a pair of moccasins for him, and we were going to hunt bears the next day.

It was just 12 o'clock when we knocked at Ebenezer's front door. Just at the moment when I should have been abstracting the $1500 from the box under the tree, according to the original proposition, Bill was counting out $250 into Dorset's hand.

When the kid found out we were going to leave him at home he started up a howl like a calliope and fastened himself as tight as a leech to Bill's leg. His father peeled him away gradually, like a porous plaster.

"How long can you hold him?" asks Bill.

"I'm not as strong as I used to be," says old Dorset, "but I think I can promise you ten minutes."

"Enough," says Bill. "In ten minutes I shall cross the central, southern, and middle western states, and be legging it trippingly for the Canadian border."

And, as dark as it was, and as fat as Bill was, and as good a runner as I am, he was a good mile and a half out of Summit before I could catch up with him.

Jane

Booth Tarkington

William's period of peculiar sensitiveness dated from that evening, and Jane, in particular, caused him a great deal of anxiety. In fact, he began to feel that Jane was a mortification which his parents might have spared him, with no loss to themselves or to the world. Not having shown that consideration for anybody, they might at least have been less spinelessly indulgent of her. William's bitter conviction was that he had never seen a child so starved of discipline or so lost to etiquette as Jane.

For one thing, her passion for bread-and-butter, covered with apple sauce and powdered sugar, was getting to be a serious matter. Secretly, William was not yet so changed by love as to be wholly indifferent to this refection himself, but his consumption of it was private, whereas Jane had formed the habit of eating it in exposed places—such as the front yard or the sidewalk. At no hour of the day was it advisable for a relative to approach the neighborhood in fastidious company, unless prepared to acknowledge kinship with a spindly young person either eating bread-and-butter and apple sauce and powdered sugar, or all too visibly just having eaten bread-and-butter and apple sauce and powdered sugar. Moreover, there were times when Jane had worse things than apple sauce to answer for, as William made clear to his mother in an oration as hot as the July noon sun which looked down upon it.

Mrs. Baxter was pleasantly engaged with a sprinkling-can and some small flower-beds in the shady back yard, and Jane, having returned from various sidewalk excursions, stood close by as a spectator, her hands replenished with the favorite food and her chin rising and falling in gentle motions, little prophecies of the slight distensions which passed down her slender throat with slow, rhythmic regularity. Upon this calm scene came William, plunging round a corner of the house, furious yet plaintive.

"You've got to do something about that child!" he began. "I *can*not stand it!"

Jane looked at him dumbly, not ceasing, however, to eat; while Mrs. Baxter thoughtfully continued her sprinkling.

"You've been gone all morning, Willie," she said. "I thought your father mentioned at breakfast that he expected you to put in at least four hours a day on your mathematics and—"

"That's neither here nor there," William returned, vehemently. "I just want to say this: if you don't do something about Jane, I will! Just look at her! *Look* at her, I ask you! That's just the way she looked half an hour ago, out on the public sidewalk in front of the house, when I came by here with Miss *Pratt*! That was pleasant, wasn't it? To be walking with a lady on the public street and meet a member of my family looking like that! Oh, *lovely*!"

In the anguish of this recollection his voice cracked, and though his eyes were dry his gestures wept for him. Plainly, he was about to reach the most lamentable portion of his narrative. "And then she *hollered* at me! She hollered, 'Oh, *Will—ee*!' " Here he gave an imitation of Jane's voice, so damnatory that Jane ceased to eat for several moments and drew herself up with a kind of dignity. "She hollered, 'Oh, *Will—ee*' at me!" he stormed. "Anybody would think I was about six years old! She hollered, 'Oh, Will—ee,' and she rubbed her stomach and slushed apple sauce all over her face, and she kept hollering, 'Will—ee!' with her mouth full. 'Will—ee, look! Good! Bread-and-butter and apple sauce and sugar! I bet you wish *you* had some, Will—ee!' "

"You did eat some, the other day," said Jane. "You ate a whole lot. You eat it every chance you get!"

"You hush up!" he shouted, and returned to his description of the outrage. "She kept *following* us! She followed us, hollering, '*Will—ee!*' till it's a wonder we didn't go deaf! And just look at her! I don't see how you can stand it to have her going around like that and people knowing it's your child! Why, she hasn't got enough *on*!"

Mrs. Baxter laughed. "Oh, for this very hot weather, I really don't think people notice or care much about—"

" 'Notice'!" he wailed. "I guess Miss *Pratt* noticed! Hot weather's no excuse for—for outright obesity!" (As Jane was thin, it is probable that William had mistaken the meaning of this word.) "Why, half o' what she *has* got on has come unfastened—especially that frightful thing hanging around her leg—and look at her back, I just beg you! I ask you to look at her back. You can see her spinal cord!"

"Column," Mrs. Baxter corrected. "Spinal column, Willie."

"What do *I* care which it is?" he fumed. "People aren't supposed to go around with it *exposed,* whichever it is! And with apple sauce on their ears!"

"There is not!" Jane protested, and at the moment when she spoke she was right. Naturally, however, she lifted her hands to the accused ears, and the unfortunate result was to justify William's statement.

"*Look!*" he cried. "I just ask you to look! Think of it: that's the sight I have to meet when I'm out walking with Miss *Pratt*! She asked me who it was, and I wish you'd seen her face. She wanted to know who 'that curious child' was, and I'm glad you didn't hear the way she said it. 'Who *is* that curious child?' she said, and I had to tell her it was my sister. I had to tell Miss *Pratt* it was my only *sister*!"

"Willie, who is Miss Pratt?" asked Mrs. Baxter, mildly. "I don't think I've ever heard of—"

Jane had returned to an admirable imperturbability, but she chose this moment to interrupt her mother, and her own eating, with remarks delivered in a tone void of emphasis or expression.

"Willie's mashed on her," she said, casually. "And she wears false side-curls. One almost came off."

At this unspeakable desecration William's face was that of a high priest stricken at the altar.

"She's visitin' Miss May Parcher," added the deadly Jane. "But the Parchers are awful tired of her. They wish she'd go home, but they don't like to tell her so."

One after another these insults from the canaille fell

upon the ears of William. That slanders so atrocious could soil the universal air seemed unthinkable.

He became icily calm.

"*Now* if you don't punish her," he said, deliberately, "it's because you have lost your sense of duty!"

Having uttered these terrible words, he turned upon his heel and marched toward the house. His mother called after him:

"Wait, Willie. Jane doesn't mean to hurt your feelings—"

"My feelings!" he cried, the iciness of his demeanor giving way under the strain of emotion. "You stand there and allow her to speak as she did of one of the —one of the—" For a moment William appeared to be at a loss, and the fact is that it always has been a difficult matter to describe *the* bright, ineffable divinity of the world to one's mother, especially in the presence of an inimical third party of tender years. "One of the—" he said; "one of the—the noblest—one of the noblest—"

Again he paused.

"Oh, Jane didn't mean anything," said Mrs. Baxter. "And if you think Miss Pratt is so nice, I'll ask May Parcher to bring her to tea with us some day. If it's too hot, we'll have iced tea, and you can ask Johnnie Watson, if you like. Don't get so upset about things, Willie!"

" 'Upset'!" he echoed, appealing to heaven against this word. " 'Upset'!" And he entered the house in a manner most dramatic.

"What made you say that?" Mrs. Baxter asked, turning curiously to Jane when William had disappeared. "Where did you hear any such things?"

"I was there," Jane replied, gently eating on and on.

William could come and William could go, but Jane's alimentary canal went on forever.

"You were where, Jane?"

"At the Parchers'."

"Oh, I see."

"Yesterday afternoon," said Jane, "when Miss Parcher had the Sunday school class for lemonade and cookies."

"Did you hear Miss Parcher say—"

"No'm," said Jane. "I ate too many cookies, I guess, maybe. Anyways, Miss Parcher said I better lay down—"

"*Lie* down, Jane."

"Yes'm. On the sofa in the liberry, an' Mrs. Parcher an' Mr. Parcher came in there an' sat down, after while, an' it was kind of dark, an' they didn't hardly notice me, or I guess they thought I was asleep, maybe. Anyways, they didn't talk loud, but Mr. Parcher would sort of grunt an' ack cross. He said he just wished he knew when he was goin' to have a home again. Then Mrs. Parcher said May *had* to ask her Sunday school class, but he said he never meant the Sunday school class. He said since Miss Pratt came to visit, there wasn't anywhere he could go, because Willie Baxter an' Johnnie Watson an' Joe Bullitt an' all the other ones like that were there all the time, an' it made him just sick at the stummick, an' he did wish there was some way to find out when she was goin' home, because he couldn't stand much more talk about love. He said Willie an' Johnnie Watson an' Joe Bullitt an' Miss Pratt were always arguin' somep'm about love, an' he said Willie was the worst. Mamma, he said he didn't like the rest of it, but he said he guessed he could stand it if it wasn't for Willie. An' he said the reason they were all so in love of Miss Pratt was because she talks baby-talk, an' he said he couldn't stand much more baby-talk. Mamma, she has the loveliest little white dog, an' Mr. Parcher doesn't like it. He said he couldn't go anywhere around the place without steppin' on the dog or Willie Baxter. An' he said he couldn't sit on his own porch any more; he said he couldn't sit even in the liberry but he had to hear baby-talk goin' on *some*wheres an' then either Willie Baxter or Joe Bullitt or somebody or another arguin' about love. Mamma, he said"—Jane became impressive—"he said mamma, he said he didn't mind the Sunday school class, but he couldn't stand those dam boys!"

"Jane!" Mrs. Baxter cried, "you *mustn't* say such things!"

"I didn't, mamma. Mr. Parcher said it. He said he couldn't stand those da—"

"*Jane!* No matter what he said, you mustn't repeat—"

"But I'm not. I only said Mr. *Parcher* said he couldn't stand those d—"

Mrs. Baxter cut the argument short by imprisoning Jane's mouth with a firm hand. Jane continued to swallow quietly until released. Then she said:

"But, mamma, how can I tell you what he said unless I say—"

"Hush!" Mrs. Baxter commanded. "You must never, never again use such a terrible and wicked word."

"I won't mamma," Jane said, meekly. Then she brightened. "Oh, *I* know! I'll say 'word' instead. Won't that be all right?"

"I—I suppose so."

"Well, Mr. Parcher said he couldn't stand those word boys. That sounds all right, doesn't it, mamma?"

Mrs. Baxter hesitated, but she was inclined to hear as complete as possible a report of Mr. and Mrs. Parcher's conversation since it seemed to concern William so nearly; and she well knew that Jane had her own way of telling things—or else they remained untold.

"I—I suppose so," Mrs. Baxter said again.

"Well, they kind of talked along," Jane continued, much pleased;—"an' Mr. Parcher said when he was young he wasn't any such a—such a word fool as these young word fools were. He said in all his born days Willie Baxter was the wordest fool he ever saw!"

Willie Baxter's mother flushed a little. "That was very unjust and very wrong of Mr. Parcher," she said, primly.

"Oh no, mamma!" Jane protested. "Mrs. Parcher thought so, too."

"Did she, indeed!"

"Only she didn't say word or wordest or anything like that," Jane explained. "She said it was because Miss Pratt had coaxed him to be so in love of her; an' Mr. Parcher said he didn't care whose fault it was, Willie was a—a word calf an' so were all the rest of 'em, Mr. Parcher said. An' he said he couldn't stand it any more. Mr. Parcher said that a whole lot of times, mamma. He said he guess' pretty soon he'd haf to be in the lunatic asylum if Miss Pratt stayed a few more days with her word little dog an' her word Willie Baxter an' all the other word calfs. Mrs. Parcher said he oughtn't to say 'word,' mamma. She said, 'Hush, hush!' to him, mamma. He talked like this mamma: he said, 'I'll be word if I stand it!' An' he kept gettin' crosser, an' he said, 'Word! Word! *Word!* WOR—' "

"There!" Mrs. Baxter interrupted, sharply. "That will do, Jane! We'll talk about something else now, I think."

Jane looked hurt; she was taking great pleasure in this confidential interview, and gladly would have continued to quote the harried Mr. Parcher at great length. Still, she was not entirely uncontent: she must have had some perception that her performance— merely as a notable bit of reportorial art—did not wholly lack style, even if her attire did. Yet, brilliant as Jane's work was, Mrs. Baxter felt no astonishment; several times ere this Jane had demonstrated a remarkable faculty for the retention of details concerning William. And running hand in hand with a really superb curiosity, this powerful memory was making Jane an even greater factor in William's life than he suspected.

During the glamors of early love, if there be a creature more deadly than the little brother of a budding woman, that creature is the little sister of a budding man. The little brother at least tells in the open all he knows, often at full power of his lungs, and even that may be avoided, since he is wax in the hands of bribery; but the little sister is more apt to save her knowledge for use upon a terrible occasion; and, no matter what bribes she may accept, she is certain to tell her mother everything. All in all, a young lover should arrange, if possible, to be the only child of elderly parents; otherwise his mother and sister are sure to know a great deal more about him than he knows that they know.

This was what made Jane's eyes so disturbing to William during lunch that day. She ate quietly and competently, but all the while he was conscious of her solemn and inscrutable gaze fixed upon him; and she spoke not once. She could not have rendered herself more annoying, especially as William was trying to treat her with silent scorn, for nothing is more irksome to the muscles of the face than silent scorn, when there is no means of showing it except by the expression. On the other hand, Jane's inscrutability gave her no discomfort whatever. In fact, inscrutability is about the most comfortable expression that a person can wear, though the truth is that just now Jane was not really inscrutable at all.

She was merely looking at William and thinking of Mr. Parcher.

Early American Gravestones

Here lies Les Moore
Killed by four slugs from a .44,
No Les, no Moore.

On a horse thief:

He found a rope and picked it up
And, with it, walked away.
It happened that, to the other end,
A horse was hitched, they say.
They took the rope and tied it up
Upon a Hickory limb.
It happened that the other end
Was somehow hitched to him.

Here lies a man who looked into the barrel
Of his gun to see if it was loaded. It was!

From the Old West:

He called Ed Smith a liar.

A National Sense of Humor

Here lies Pecos Bill.
He always lied and always will.
He once lied loud.
He now lies still.

He was young, he was fair,
But the Injuns raised his hair.

Here lie the remains of poor Christopher Type.
The rest of him couldn't be found.
He sat on a powder cask smoking his pipe.
Now the wind blows his ashes around.

It was a cough that carried him off.
It was a coffin they carried him off in.

Alas, friend Joseph,
His death was sudden
As though the mandate
Came straight from heaven.
His foot did slip, and he did fall.
"Help, help," he cried, and that was all.

To all my friends I bid adieu.
A quicker death I never knew.
As I was leading my horse to drink,
She kicked and killed me quick as a wink.

Here, under this sod and these very trees,
Is buried the body of Soloman Pease,
But here in this hole lies only his pod.
His soul is shelled out and gone to God.

Here lies the body of Jonathan Near,
Whose mouth, it stretched from ear to ear.
Tread softly, stranger, o'er this wonder,
For if he yawns, you're gone, by thunder.

4.

1920-1929

Roaring with Laughter

Cartoon—Eldon Kelley
Comic Strip—Winnie Winkle
Alibi Ike—Ring Lardner
Dr. Kronkhite—Smith and Dale
Why a Duck?—Marx Brothers
Knock, Knock Jokes

Introduction

In the period following World War I, it was clear that the United States was no longer a land of farmers and shopkeepers, but a wealthy and powerful nation that had "arrived."

Improvements in technical and scientific knowledge led to new and faster methods of communication. Mechanical typesetting speeded up the printing of books, magazines, and newspapers; and so more reading material was available to a greater number of people.

The new automobiles and airplanes were taken advantage of by many travellers and this stimulated a tremendous growth in the transportation industry. Now vaudeville troups and musical comedy companies were able to journey rapidly from one town to another, and "Next Stop, East Lynn," became an easy reality.

The invention of the silent movie enabled Americans in every state to laugh at what they were *seeing* on the screen. In Charlie Chaplin's "little man," in the routines of the Marx Brothers, in the productions of Mack Sennett, our tendency to poke fun at pompous, conceited, and greedy people found visual expression. This new brand of humor was called "*slapstick*. And another visual way of expressing humor was introduced in the cartoon, now added to comic strips and joke columns in newspapers and magazines.

Children now attended school for a longer time; adult immigrants imparted to new neighbors their reverence for education. Since education and reading go together, humor found still another outlet: in comedy in language, or fun with words, and word games.

"My dear, your skirt is positively *dra*gging!"

ELDON KELLEY   —1928

Martin Branner, "Winnie Winkle," 1927.

Alibi Ike

Ring Lardner

His right name was Frank X. Farrell, and I guess the X stood for "Excuse me." Because he never pulled a play, good or bad, on or off the field, without apologizin' for it.

"Alibi Ike" was the name Carey wished on him the first day he reported down South. O' course we all cut out the "Alibi" part of it right away for the fear he would overhear it and bust somebody. But we called him "Ike" right to his face and the rest of it was understood by everybody on the club except Ike himself.

He ast me one time, he says:

"What do you all call me Ike for? I ain't no Yid."

"Carey give you the name," I says. "It's his nickname for everybody he takes a likin' to."

"He mustn't have only a few friends then," says Ike. "I never heard him say 'Ike' to nobody else."

But I was goin' to tell you about Carey namin' him. We'd been workin' out two weeks and the pitchers was showin' somethin' when this bird joined us. His first day out he stood up there so good and took such a reef at the old pill that he had everyone lookin'. Then him and Carey was together in left field, catchin' fungoes,

and it was after we was through for the day that Carey
told me about him.

"What do you think of Alibi Ike?" ast Carey.

"Who's that?" I says.

"This here Farrell in the outfield," says Carey.

"He looks like he could hit," I says.

"Yes," says Carey, "but he can't hit near as good as
he can apologize."

Then Carey went on to tell me what Ike had been
pullin' out there. He'd dropped the first fly ball that
was hit to him and told Carey his glove wasn't broke in
good yet, and Carey says the glove could easy of been
Kid Gleason's gran'father. He made a whale of a catch
out o' the next one and Carey says "Nice work!" or
somethin' like that, but Ike says he could of caught the
ball with his back turned only he slipped when he
started after it and, besides that, the air currents fooled
him.

"I thought you done well to get to the ball," says
Carey.

"I ought to been settin' under it," says Ike.

"What did you hit last year?" Carey ast him.

"I had malaria most o' the season," says Ike. "I
wound up with .356."

"Where would I have to go to get malaria?" says
Carey, but Ike didn't wise up.

I and Carey and him set at the same table together
for supper. It took him half an hour longer'n us to eat
because he had to excuse himself every time he lifted
his fork.

"Doctor told me I needed starch," he'd say, and
then toss a shovelful o'potatoes into him. Or, "They

ain't much meat on one o' these chops," he'd tell us, and grab another one. Or he'd say: "Nothin' like onions for a cold," and then he'd dip into the perfumery.

"Better try that apple sauce," says Carey. "It'll help your malaria."

"Whose malaria?" says Ike. He'd forgot already why he didn't only hit .356 last year.

I and Carey begin to lead him on.

"Whereabouts did you say your home was?" I ast him.

"I live with my folks," he says. "We live in Kansas City—not right down in the business part—outside a ways."

"How's that come?" says Carey. "I should think you'd get rooms in the post office."

But Ike was too busy curin' his cold to get that one.

"Are you married?" I ast him.

"No," he says. "I never run round much with girls, except to shows onct in a wile and parties and dances and roller skatin'."

"Never take 'em to the prize fights, eh?" says Carey.

"We don't have no real good bouts," says Ike. "Just bush stuff. And I never figured a boxin' match was a place for the ladies."

Well, after supper he pulled a cigar out and lit it. I was just goin' to ask him what he done it for, but he beat me to it.

"Kind o' rests a man to smoke after a good workout," he says. "Kind o' settles a man's supper, too."

"Looks like a pretty good cigar," says Carey.

"Yes," says Ike. "A friend o' mine give it to me—a fella in Kansas City that runs a billiard room."

"Do you play billiards?" I ast him.

"I used to play a fair game," he says. "I'm all out o' practice now—can't hardly make a shot."

We coaxed him into a four-handed battle, him and Carey against Jack Mack and I. Say, he couldn't play billiards as good as Willie Hoppe; not quite. But to hear him tell it, he didn't make a good shot all evenin'. I'd leave him an awful-lookin' layout and he'd gather 'em up in one try and then run a couple o' hundred, and between every carom he'd say he'd put too much stuff on the ball, or the English didn't take, or the table wasn't true, or his stick was crooked, or somethin'. And all the time he had the balls actin' like they was Dutch soldiers and him Kaiser William. We started out to play fifty points, but we had to make it a thousand so as I and Jack and Carey could try the table.

The four of us set round the lobby a wile after we was through playin', and when it got along toward bedtime Carey whispered to me and says:

"Ike'd like to go to bed, but he can't think up no excuse."

Carey hadn't hardly finished whisperin' when Ike got up and pulled it:

"Well, good night boys," he says. "I ain't sleepy, but I got some gravel in my shoes and it's killin' my feet."

We knowed he hadn't never left the hotel since we'd came in from the grounds and changed our clo'es. So Carey says:

"I should think they'd take them gravel pits out o' the billiard room."

But Ike was already on his way to the elevator, limpin'.

"He's got the world beat," says Carey to Jack and I.

"I've knew lots o' guys that had an alibi for every mistake they made; I've heard pitchers say that the ball slipped when somebody cracked one off'n 'em; I've heard infielders complain of a sore arm after heavin' one into the stand, and I've saw outfielders tooken sick with a dizzy spell when they've misjudged a fly ball. But this baby can't even go to bed without apologizin', and I bet he excuses himself to the razor when he gets ready to shave."

"And at that," says Jack, "he's goin' to make us a good man."

"Yes," says Carey, "unless rheumatism keeps his battin' average down to .400."

Well, sir, Ike kept whalin' away at the ball all through the trip till everybody knowed he'd won a job. Cap had him in there regular the last few exhibition games and told the newspaper boys a week before the season opened that he was goin' to start him in Kane's place.

"You're there, kid," says Carey to Ike, the night Cap made the 'nnouncement. "They ain't many boys that wins a big league berth their third year out."

"I'd of been up here a year ago," says Ike, "only I was bent over all season with lumbago."

II

It rained down in Cincinnati one day and somebody organized a little game o' cards. They was shy two men to make six and ast I and Carey to play.

"I'm with you if you get Ike and make it seven-handed," says Carey.

So they got a hold of Ike and we went up to Smitty's room.

"I pretty near forgot how many you deal," says Ike. "It's been a long wile since I played."

I and Carey give each other the wink, and sure enough, he was just as ig'orant about poker as billiards. About the second hand, the pot was opened two or three ahead of him, and they was three in when it come his turn. It cost a buck, and he throwed in two.

"It's raised, boys," somebody says.

"Gosh, that's right, I did raise it," says Ike.

"Take out a buck if you didn't mean to tilt her," says Carey.

"No," says Ike, "I'll leave it go."

Well, it was raised back at him and then he made another mistake and raised again. They was only three left in when the draw come. Smitty'd opened with a pair o' kings and he didn't help 'em. Ike stood pat. The guy that'd raised him back was flushin' and he didn't fill. So Smitty checked and Ike bet and didn't get no call. He tossed his hand away, but I grabbed it and give it a look. He had king, queen, jack and two tens. Alibi Ike he must have seen me peekin', for he leaned over and whispered to me.

"I overlooked my hand," he says. "I thought all the wile it was a straight."

"Yes," I says, "that's why you raised twice by mistake."

They was another pot that he come into with tens and fours. It was tilted a couple o' times and two o' the strong fellas drawed ahead of Ike. They each drawed one. So Ike throwed away his little pair and come out

with four tens. And they was four treys against him.
Carey'd looked at Ike's discards and then he says:

"This lucky bum busted two pair."

"No, no, I didn't," says Ike.

"Yes, yes, you did," says Carey, and showed us the
two fours.

"What do you know about that?" says Ike. "I'd of
swore one was a five spot."

Well, we hadn't had no pay day yet, and after a wile
everybody except Ike was goin' shy. I could see him
gettin' restless and I was wonderin' how he'd make the
get-away. He tried two or three times. "I got to buy
some collars before supper," he says.

"No hurry," says Smitty. "The stores here keeps
open all night in April."

After a minute he opened up again.

"My uncle out in Nebraska ain't expected to live,"
he says. "I ought to send a telegram."

"Would that save him?" says Carey.

"No, it sure wouldn't," says Ike, "but I ought to
leave my old man know where I'm at."

"When did you hear about your uncle?" says Carey.

"Just this mornin'," says Ike.

"Who told you?" ast Carey.

"I got a wire from my old man," says Ike.

"Well," says Carey, "your old man knows you're
still here yet this afternoon if you was here this mornin'. Trains leavin' Cincinnati in the middle o' the day
don't carry no ball clubs."

"Yes," says Ike, "that's true. But he don't know
where I'm goin' to be next week."

"Ain't he got no schedule?" ast Carey.

"I sent him one openin' day," says Ike, "but it takes mail a long time to get to Idaho."

"I thought your old man lived in Kansas City," says Carey.

"He does when he's home," says Ike.

"But now," says Carey, "I s'pose he's went to Idaho so as he can be near your sick uncle in Nebraska."

"He's visitin' my other uncle in Idaho."

"Then how does he keep posted about your sick uncle?" ast Carey.

"He don't," says Ike. "He don't even know my other uncle's sick. That's why I ought to wire and tell him."

"Good night!" says Carey.

"What town in Idaho is your old man at?" I says.

Ike thought it over.

"No town at all," he says. "But he's near a town."

"Near what town?" I says.

"Yuma," says Ike.

Well, by this time he'd lost two or three pots and he was desperate. We was playin' just as fast as we could, because we seen we couldn't hold him much longer. But he was tryin' so hard to frame an escape that he couldn't pay no attenton to the cards, and it looked like we'd get his whole pile away from him if we could make him stick.

The telephone saved him. The minute it begun to ring, five of us jumped for it. But Ike was there first.

"Yes," he says, answerin' it. "This is him. I'll come right down."

And he slammed up the receiver and beat it out o' the door without even sayin' good-by.

"Smitty'd ought to locked the door," says Carey.

"What did he win?" ast Carey.

We figured it up—sixty-odd bucks.

"And the next time we ask him to play," says Carey, "his fingers will be so stiff he can't hold the cards."

Well, we set round a while talkin' it over, and pretty soon the telephone rung again. Smitty answered it. It was a friend of his'n from Hamilton and he wanted to know why Smitty didn't hurry down. He was the one that had called before and Ike had told him he was Smitty.

"Ike'd ought to split with Smitty's friend," says Carey.

"No," I says, "he'll need all he won. It costs money to buy collars and to send telegrams from Cincinnati to your old man in Texas and keep him posted on the health o' your uncle in Cedar Rapids, D.C."

Dr. Kronkhite

Smith and Dale
A Vaudeville Classic

PATIENT: *(Enters doctor's office)*

NURSE: How do you do.

PATIENT: This is doctor Kronkhite's office, no?

NURSE: Yes. I'm his nurse.

PATIENT: Is the doctor sick too?

NURSE: No. I'm a trained nurse.

PATIENT: Oh. You do tricks. . . . Is the doctor in?

NURSE: Yes, but he's very busy.

PATIENT: I'll wait.

NURSE: Take a chair please.

PATIENT: Thank you. I'll take it on my way out . . . what's the doctor's office hours?

NURSE: They're from 12 to 3 . . . 3 to 6 . . . 6 to 9 . . . 9 to 12 . . . and 12 to 3.

PATIENT: He gives good odds, he must be a horse doctor.

NURSE: Those are his hours.

PATIENT: Is the doctor a good doctor?

NURSE: He'll do you good.

VOICE: *(Off stage we hear loud groans)* Oh you butcher!

PATIENT: I'm cured. *(Starts to leave but nurse stops him)*

NURSE: Where are you going?

PATIENT: I'm going home. I forgot something.

NURSE: What did you forget?

PATIENT: I forgot to stay home.

NURSE: You mustn't run out on the doctor.

PATIENT: Better than being carried out! *(Nurse exits)*

DOCTOR: *(Enters. Skips over to patient)* How do you do sir.

PATIENT: *(A bit skeptical)* Are you a doctor?

DOCTOR: Yes.

PATIENT: I'm dubious.

DOCTOR: How do you do Mr. Dubious. Sit down Mr. Dubious.

DOCTOR: Mr. Dubious, are you married?

PATIENT: Yes, and no.

DOCTOR: What do you mean, yes and no.

PATIENT: I am, but I wish I wasn't . . . you see I'm my wife's step-husband. He stepped out, and I stepped in.

DOCTOR: You carry any insurance?

PATIENT: Not one penny.

DOCTOR: If you should kick the bucket, what'll your wife bury you with?

PATIENT: With pleasure.

DOCTOR: Well, that's that. Now, what's the matter with you?

PATIENT: I'm as sick as a dog.

DOCTOR: You came to the right place. I'm also a veterinarian.

PATIENT: Where did you practice?

DOCTOR: I practiced in Cairo.

PATIENT: A chiropracticer too . . . which are you going to practice on me?

DOCTOR: What's your complaint?

PATIENT: Every time I eat a heavy meal I don't feel so hungry after.

DOCTOR: Maybe you're not eating the right kind of vitaminnies. What kind of dishes do you eat?

PATIENT: Dishes? what am I a crockadile?

DOCTOR: What do you do for exercise?

PATIENT: I ride horseback every midnight.

DOCTOR: Why do you pick such an hour?

PATIENT: In the daytime the crook who owns the horse wants six dollars an hour.

DOCTOR: What does he charge at night?

PATIENT: He isn't there.

DOCTOR: What kind of meats do you eat?

PATIENT: Weal I eat.

DOCTOR: I don't ask you will you eat, I said what do you eat?

PATIENT: I told you weal. *(Spells)* We-he-hay-hell. Weal.

DOCTOR: You should say we with a v instead of a woo. Now, how do you like your veal well to do?

PATIENT: It could be medium on one side and optional on the other.

DOCTOR: So far so good. Now when you are drinking drinks what kind of beverage drinks you are drinking?

PATIENT: You mean like coffee, milk, or chocolate?

DOCTOR: Yes.

PATIENT: I drink tea. And strong tea is my weakness.

DOCTOR: You drink Ceylion tea?

PATIENT: No. Orange Peconeeze. Ouch!

DOCTOR: What troubles you?

PATIENT: Bursitis and it's on the back of my neck. That's a bad place.

DOCTOR: Where would you want a better place than on the back of your neck?

PATIENT: On the back of your neck . . . and I got a corn on the bottom of my foot. That's a bad spot, no?

DOCTOR: Yes it's a good spot because nobody can step on it but you. Now, regarding your bursitis you should go to Mount Clemmons.

PATIENT: Is that a good place for bursitis?

DOCTOR: The best place in the country.

PATIENT: How do you know?

DOCTOR: That's where I got mine . . . or you can go to Switzerland.

PATIENT: What can I do in Switzerland?

DOCTOR: Just sit there and switz . . . now, take off the coat my boy I want to diogenes the case.

PATIENT: *(Removes coat puts it across the chair)*

DOCTOR: *(Sings while he takes out his stethoscope . . . he blows his breath on the handles and rubs it with his bandana 'kerchief)*

PATIENT: Doctor. What are you doing?

DOCTOR: I'm sterlizing the instrument. *(He places the stethoscope to the patient's chest)* Now. Don't breath . . . I would like to see you inhale . . . *(Listens)* Inhale! I would like to see you.

PATIENT: *(Surprised)* Inhale I would like to see YOU!

DOCTOR: Now keep your mouth open and say, FISH.

PATIENT: *(With open mouth)* Herring.

DOCTOR: Stick out your tongue.

PATIENT: *(Does so)*

DOCTOR: More! more!

PATIENT: I can't, it's tied on the back.

DOCTOR: *(Looks at it)*

PATIENT: Well?

DOCTOR: I've seen better tongues hanging in a delicatessen window. Now, how do you sleep?

PATIENT: *(Closes eyes and crosses arms)* Like this.

DOCTOR: You don't get me.

PATIENT: I don't want you.

DOCTOR: *(Jumps up and down)* Please! Don't aggravate me. I got no patience.

PATIENT: I shouldn't be here either.

DOCTOR: I asked you how do you sleep at night?

PATIENT: At night I can't sleep. I walk around all night.

DOCTOR: Oh. You're a sonnambulance.

PATIENT: No. I'm a night watchman.

DOCTOR: Now sit down, close your eyes, and throw out your face.

PATIENT: *(Puzzled)* Throw it out?

DOCTOR: Throw out your face!

PATIENT: Did you ever take a good look at *your* face?

DOCTOR: *(Jumps up and down)* For pity sake! You are crazy!

PATIENT: I'm crazy for coming here and don't take advantage of me because I'm sick.

DOCTOR: You got sick. I didn't send for you . . . now, look me in the face.

PATIENT: I got my own troubles.

DOCTOR: Alright you can put your coat on.

PATIENT: You understand the whole case.

DOCTOR: Yes. The trouble with you is you need eyeglasses.

PATIENT: What do I owe you?

DOCTOR: Ten dollars.

PATIENT: For what?

DOCTOR: Ten dollars for my advice.

PATIENT: Here's two dollars. Take it doctor. That's my advice.

DOCTOR: You're nothing but a cheap low-down addlepated first-class insignificant . . .

PATIENT: *(Still holding the bills in front of the doctor)* One more word from you and you'll only get a dollar.

DOCTOR: YOU . . .

PATIENT: That's the word. Here's the dollar . Good-by.

Why A Duck?

Marx Brothers

From the Movie Classic

GROUCHO: Well, I'll show you how you can make some REAL money. I'm going to hold an auction in a little while in Cocoanut Manor. You—you know what an auction is, eh?

CHICO: I come from Italy on the Atlantic-Auction.

GROUCHO: Well, let's go ahead as if nothing happened. I say I'm holding an auction at Cocoanut Manor. And when the crowd gathers around, I want you to mingle with them. Don't pick their pockets, just mingle with them—and—.

CHICO: I'll find time for both.

GROUCHO: Well, maybe we can cut out the auction. Here's what I mean. If somebody says a hundred dollars, you say two—if somebody says two hundred dollars, you say three—

CHICO: Speaka up?

GROUCHO: That's right. Now, if nobody says anything, then you start it off.

CHICO: How'm I going to know when to no say nuthin'?

GROUCHO: Well, they'll probably notify you. You fool, if they don't say anything, you'll hear 'em, won't you?

CHICO: Well, mebbe I no lissen.

GROUCHO: Well, don't tell 'em. Now then, if we're successful in disposing of these lots, I'll see that you get a nice commission.

CHICO: How about some money?

GROUCHO: Well, you can have your choice.

GROUCHO: Now, in arranging these lots, of course, we use blue prints. You know what a blue print is, huh?

CHICO: OYSTERS!

GROUCHO: How is it that you never got double pneumonia?

CHICO: I go around by myself.

GROUCHO: Do you know what a lot is?

CHICO: Yeah, too much.

GROUCHO: I don't mean a whole lot. Just a little lot with nothing on it.

CHICO: Any time you gotta too much, you gotta whole lot. Look, I'll explain it to you. Some time you no gotta much; sometimes you gotta whole lot. You know that it's a lot. Somebody else maybe thinka it's too much; it's a whole lot, too. Now, a whole lot is too much; too much is a whole lot; same thing.

GROUCHO: Come here, Rand McNally, and I'll explain this thing to you. Now look, this is a map and diagram of the whole Cocoanut section. This whole area is within a radius of approximately three-quarters of a mile. Radius? Is there a remote possibility that you know what a radius means?

CHICO: It'sa WJZ.

GROUCHO: Well—I walked right into that one. It's going to be a cinch explaining the rest of this thing to you—I can see that.

CHICO: I catcha on quick.

GROUCHO: That's a rodeo you're thinking of. Look, Einstein. Here's Cocoanut Manor. No matter what you say, this is Cocoanut Manor. Here's Cocoanut Manor. Here's Cocoanut Heights. That's a swamp— right over where the—where the road forks, that's Cocoanut Junction.

CHICO: Where have you got Cocoanut Custard?

GROUCHO: Why, that's on one of the forks. You probably eat with your knife, so you wouldn't have to worry about that.

GROUCHO: Now, here's the main road, leading out of Cocoanut Manor. That's the road I wish you were on. Now over here—on this site we're going to build an Eye and Ear Hospital. This is going to be a sight for sore eyes. You understand? That's fine. Now, right here is the residential section.

CHICO: People live there, eh?

GROUCHO: No, that's the stockyard. Now all along here—this is the river front—all along the river, all along the river—those are levees.

CHICO: Thatsa the Jewish neighborhood.

GROUCHO: Well, we'll pass over that.

GROUCHO: You're a peach, boy! Now, here is a little peninsula, and here is a viaduct leading over to the mainland.

CHICO: Why a duck?

GROUCHO: I'm all right. How are you? I say here is a little peninsula, and here's a viaduct leading over to the mainland.

CHICO: All right. Why a duck?

GROUCHO: I'm not playing Ask-Me-Another. I say, that's a viaduct.

CHICO: All right. Why a duck? Why a—why a duck? Why-a-no-chicken?

GROUCHO: I don't know why-a-no-chicken. I'm a stranger here myself. All I know is that it's a viaduct. You try to cross over there a chicken, and you'll find out why a duck. It's deep water, that's viaduct.

CHICO: That's-why-a-duct?

GROUCHO: Look . . . Suppose you were out horseback riding and you came to that stream and wanted to ford over there, you couldn't make it. Too deep.

CHICO: But what do you want with a Ford when you gotta horse?

GROUCHO: Well, I'm sorry the matter ever came up. All I know is that it's a viaduct.

CHICO: No look . . . all righta . . . I catcha on to why-a-horse, why-a-chicken, why-a-this, why-a-that. I no catch on to why-a-duck.

GROUCHO: I was only fooling. I was only fooling. They're going to build a tunnel in the morning. Now, is that clear to you?

CHICO: Yes. Everything—excepta why-a-duck.

GROUCHO: Well, that's fine. Now I can go ahead. Now, look, I'm going to take you down and show you our cemetery. I've got a waiting list of fifty people at the cemetery just dying to get in. But I like you—

CHICO: —Ah—you're-a-my friend.

GROUCHO: I like you and I'm going—

CHICO: I know you like-a . . .

GROUCHO: To shove you in ahead of all of them. I'm going to see that you get a steady position.

CHICO: That's good.

GROUCHO: And if I can arrange it, it will be horizontal.

CHICO: Yeah, I see—

GROUCHO: Now remember, when the auction starts, if anybody says one hundred dollars—

CHICO: I-a say-a two hundred—

GROUCHO: That's grand. Now, if somebody says two hundred—

CHICO: —I-a say three hundred!

GROUCHO: That's great!

GROUCHO: Yes. Now, you know how to get down there?

CHICO: No, I no understand.

GROUCHO: Now, look. Listen. You go down there, down to that narrow path there, until you come to the—to the little jungle there. You see it? Where those thatched palms were?

CHICO: Yes, I see.

GROUCHO: And the, there's a little clearing there, a little clearing with a wire fence around it. You see that wire fence there?

CHICO: All right. Why-a-fence?

GROUCHO: Oh no, we're not going to go all through that again! You come along with me, and I'll fix you up!

Knock, Knock Jokes

Knock, knock.
Who's there?
Cigarette.
Cigarette who?
Cigarette life if you don't weaken.

Knock, knock.
Who's there?
Amos.
Amos who?
A mosquito bit me.

Knock, knock.
Who's there?
Max.
Max who?
Max no difference.

Knock, knock.
Who's there?
Sarah.
Sarah who?
Sarah doctor in the house?

157

Knock, knock.
Who's there?
Yule.
Yule who?
Yule never know.

Knock, knock.
Who's there?
Eileen.
Eileen who?
Eileen down to tie my shoe.

Knock, knock.
Who's there?
Window.
Window who?
Window we eat?

Knock, knock.
Who's there?
Avenue.
Avenue who?
Avenue a baby sister?

Knock, knock.
Who's there?
Tarzan.
Tarzan who?
Tarzan stripes forever.

Knock, knock.
Who's there?
Cargo.
Cargo who?
Cargo honk, honk.

5.

1930-1939

Looking Back Laughing

Cartoon—J. R. Williams

Another Uncle Edith Christmas Story—Robert Benchley

The Night the Bed Fell—James Thurber

Father Opens My Mail—Clarence Day

Pencil-Chewing—Frank Sullivan

Who's on First?—Abbott and Costello

She Was Only Jokes

Introduction

The Thirties were years of economic depression and hardship for a people faced with the complexities of everyday living in an increasingly industrialized and gadget-minded society. Humor, less spontaneous and more commercialized, became an industry on its own. New books and magazines came out that were devoted exclusively to humor, to cartoons, to light verse. In radio and film (the "talkies" were now being shown) comedy situations were exploited more and more.

American humor continued its oral tradition, in which stories and jokes passed from mouth to mouth, from generation to generation. Meanwhile, humorists such as Robert Benchley and James Thurber were a new breed. They were educated, sophisticated, and literate, and their work appeared in all the media available to comedy—plays, movies, radio, magazine articles, and cartoons. Output was large, although this type of professional humorist was rare.

But with the country's greater exposure to comedy, appetite for it increased geometrically. There were more movie houses, with more movies showing in them, more comic radio shows, more vaudeville acts, and more humor magazines. Always more.

J. R. WILLIAMS

Another Uncle Edith Christmas Story

Robert Benchley

Uncle Edith said, "I think it is about time that I told you a good old-fashioned Christmas story about the raging sea."

"Aw, nuts!" said little Philip.

"As you will," said Uncle Edith, "but I shall tell it just the same. I am not to be intimidated by a three-year-old child. Where was I?"

"You were over backwards, with your feet in the air, if I know anything about you," said Marian, who had golden hair and wore it in an unbecoming orange ribbon.

"I guess that you probably are right," said Uncle Edith, "although who am I to say? Anyway, I *do* know that we sailed from Nahant on the fourteenth March."

"What are you—French?" asked little Philip. "The fourteenth March."

"The fourteenth *of* March, then," said Uncle Edith, "and if you don't shut up I will keep right on with the story. You can't intimidate me."

"Done and done," said little Philip, who bled quite a lot from a wound in his head inflicted a few seconds before by Uncle Edith.

"We set sail from Nahant on the fourteenth *of* March (nya-a-a-a-a) on the good ship *Patience W.*

Littbaum, with a cargo of old thread and bound for Algeciras."

"End of story!" announced Marian in a throaty baritone.

"It is *not* the end of the story, and I will sue anyone who says that it is," petulated Uncle Edith. "You will know well enough when I come to the end of the story, because I shall fall over on my face. Now be quiet or Uncle Edith will give you a great big abrasion on the forehead."

"I can hardly wait," said little Philip, or whichever the hell one of those children it was. I can't keep them all straight, they are all so much alike.

"Aboard," continued Uncle Edith, "aboard were myself, as skipper—"

"Skippered herring," (*a whisper*).

"—Lars Jannssenn, first mate; Max Schnirr, second mate; Enoch Olds, third base; and a crew of seven whose names you wouldn't recognize. However, there we were.

"The first seven hundred and nine days were uneventful. The sailmaker (a man by the name of Sailmaker, oddly enough) made eleven sails, but, as we had no more ships to put them on, and as our sails were O.K., we had to throw them overboard. This made the men discontented, and there were rumors of mutiny. I sent a reporter up to see the men, however, and the rumors were unconfirmed; so I killed the story. NO MUTINY was the head I put on it in the ship's paper that night, and everybody was satisfied."

"You great big wonderful animal," said Marian, running her tiny hand through Uncle Edith's hair.

"It was nothing," said Uncle Edith, and everybody agreed that it certainly was.

"However," continued the old salt pork, "everyone on board felt that something was wrong. We were at that time at Lat. seventy-eight, Long. seventy-eight, which cancelled each other, making us right back where we started from—"

"Don't tell me that we are back at Nahant again," said little Philip, throwing up.

"Not exactly Nahant," said Uncle Edith, "but within hailing distance of a Nahanted ship."

"You just used Nahant in the first place so that you could pull that gag," said Primrose, who, up to this time, had taken no part in the conversation, not having been born.

"So help me God," said Uncle Edith, "it came to me like *that*!" And he snapped a finger, breaking it. "The ha'nted ship lay just off our starboard bow, and seemed to be manned by mosquitoes. As we drew alongside, however, we found that there was not a soul on board. Not a soul on board."

"That is the second time you have said that," said little whatever-his-name-is—Philip.

Uncle Edith made no reply other than to throw nasty little Philip into irons.

" 'Prepare to board!' was the order given. And everybody, ignoring the chance for a pun, prepared to board the derelict. In a few seconds we were swarming over the side of the empty ship and searching every nook and cranny of her. The search, however, was fruitless. The ship's log was found in the wheelhouse, but, as the last entry read, 'Fair and warm. Billy said he didn't love me as much as he does Anna' we discarded that as evidence. In the galley we found a fried egg, done on only one side, and an old bo'sun who was no good to anybody. Other than these two things, the mystery was complete."

"Not that I give a damn," said Marian, "but what was the explanation to this almost complete mystery?"

"If you will shut your trap," said Uncle Edith, "I will tell you. As I may not have told you, the mystery ship was full of sleeping Hessian troops, such as were used against the colonists in the Revolutionary War. They were very gay in their red coats and powdered wigs, and, had they been awake, might have offered some solution of the problem which now presented itself to us.

" 'What shall I do, cap'n?' asked Lars Jannssenn, who had been promoted to purser.

" 'What would you *like* to do, Lars?' I asked him.

" 'Me, I would like to have three wishes,' was the typically Scandinavian reply. (Lars had belonged to the Scandi-navy before he joined up with us.)

" 'They are yours,' I said, more on the spur of the moment than anything else. 'You take your three wishes and put them in your hat and pull it down over your ears. Anybody else?'

"Suddenly there was a scream from below decks. I have heard screams in my day, but never anything like this one. It was dark by now, and there were a lot of couples necking in the lifeboats. But this scream was different. It was like nothing human. It came from the bowels of the ship, and you know that's bad.

" 'All hands below!' I cried, and just as everybody was rushing down the hatchways there came a great explosion, seemingly from the jib.

" 'All hands to the jib!' I cried in my excitement.

" 'What is all this—a game?' asked the crew, as one man.

" 'I am captain here,' I said, boxing the compass roundly, 'and what I say goes! In the future please try to remember that fact.'

"Well, this sort of thing went on for hours. Up and down that ship we went, throwing overboard Hessians in our rush, until finally the cook came to me and said, 'Cap'n, I frankly am sick of this. Are there, or are there not, any reasons why we should be behaving like a pack of schoolboys?'

"This was a poser. I called the crew together and we decided to go back to the *Patience W. Littbaum*. But, on looking over the side, we found a very suspicious circumstance. *The Patience W. Littbaum was gone!*"

"I don't believe it!" said little Philip, from the brig.

Uncle Edith turned sharply. "I thought you were in irons" he said.

"You think a lot," replied little Philip, and the entire casino burst into a gale of laughter, although it was a pretty lousy comeback, even for a three-year-old.

"Very well, then," said Uncle Edith. "I am sorry if you feel that way. For I was just going to end the story by saying that we sailed the mystery ship back to Nahant."

"And where does Christmas come in?" piped up Marian, who hadn't heard a word of Uncle Edith's story.

"Who the hell said anything about Christmas?" asked Uncle Edith in a rage.

And who the hell did?

The Night the Bed Fell

James Thurber

I suppose that the high-water mark of my youth in Columbus, Ohio, was the night the bed fell on my father. It makes a better recitation (unless, as some friends of mine have said, one has heard it five or six times) then it does a piece of writing, for it is almost necessary to throw furniture around, shake doors, and bark like a dog, to lend the proper atmosphere and verisimilitude to what is admittedly a somewhat incredible tale. Still, it did take place.

It happened, then, that my father had decided to sleep in the attic one night, to be away where he could think. My mother opposed the notion strongly because, she said, the old wooden bed up there was unsafe: it was wobbly and the heavy headboard would crash down on father's head in case the bed fell, and kill him. There was no dissuading him, however, and at a quarter past ten he closed the attic door behind him and went up the narrow twisting stairs. We later heard ominous creakings as he crawled into bed. Grandfather, who usually slept in the attic bed when he was with us, had disappeared some days before. (On these occasions he was usually gone six or eight days and returned growling and out of temper, with the news that the federal Union was run by a passel of blockheads and that the Army of the Potomac didn't have any more chance than a fiddler's bitch.)

We had visiting us at this time a nervous first cousin of mine named Briggs Beall, who believed that he was likely to cease breathing when he was asleep. It was his feeling that if he were not awakened every hour during the night, he might die of suffocation. He had been accustomed to setting an alarm clock to ring at intervals until morning, but I persuaded him to abandon this. He slept in my room and I told him that I was such a light sleeper that if anybody quit breathing in the same room with me, I would wake instantly. He tested me the first night—which I had suspected he would—by holding his breath after my regular breathing had convinced him I was asleep. I was not asleep, however, and called to him. This seemed to allay his fears a little, but he took the precaution of putting a glass of spirits of camphor on a little table at the head of his bed. In case I didn't arouse him until he was almost gone, he said, he would sniff the camphor, a powerful reviver. Briggs was not the only member of his family who had his crotchets. Old Aunt Melissa Beall (who could whistle like a man, with two fingers in her mouth) suffered under the premonition that she was destined to die on South High Street, because she had been born on South High Street and married on South High Street. Then there was Aunt Sarah Shoaf, who never went to bed at night without the fear that a burglar was going to get in and blow chloroform under her door through a tube. To avert this calamity—for she was in greater dread of anesthetics than of losing her household goods—she always piled her money, silverware, and other valuables in a neat stack just outside her bedroom, with a note reading: "This is all I have. Please take it and do not use your chloroform, as this is all I have." Aunt Gracie Shoaf also had a burglar phobia, but she met it with more fortitude. She was confident that burglars had been getting into her house every night for forty years. The fact that she never missed anything was to her no proof to the contrary. She always claimed that she scared them off before they could take anything, by throwing shoes down the hallway. When she went to bed she piled, where she could get at them handily, all the shoes there were about her house. Five minutes after she had turned off the light, she would sit up in bed and say "Hark!" Her husband, who had learned to ignore the whole situation as long ago as 1903, would either be sound asleep or pretend to be sound asleep. In either case he would not respond to her tugging and pulling, so that presently she would arise, tiptoe to the door, open it slightly and heave a shoe down the hall in one direction and its mate down the hall in the other direction. Some nights she threw them all, some nights only a couple of pair.

But I am straying from the remarkable incidents that took place during the night that the bed fell on father. By midnight we were all in bed. The layout of the rooms and the disposition of their occupants is important to an understanding of what later occurred. In the front room upstairs (just under father's attic bedroom) were my mother and my brother Herman, who sometimes sang in his sleep, usually "Marching Through Georgia" or "Onward, Christian Soldiers." Briggs Beall and myself were in a room adjoining this one. My brother Roy was in a room across the hall from ours. Our bull terrier Rex slept in the hall.

My bed was an army cot, one of those affairs which are made wide enough to sleep on comfortably only by putting up, flat with the middle section, the two sides which ordinarily hang down like the sideboards of a drop-leaf table. When these sides are up, it is perilous to roll too far toward the edge, for then the cot is likely to tip completely over, bringing the whole bed down on top of one with a tremendous banging crash. This, in fact, is precisely what happened, about two o'clock in the morning. (It was my mother who, in recalling the scene later, first referred to it as "the night the bed fell on your father.")

Always a deep sleeper, slow to arouse (I had lied to Briggs), I was at first unconscious of what had happened when the iron cot rolled me onto the floor and toppled over on me. It left me still warmly bundled up and unhurt, for the bed rested above me like a canopy. Hence I did not wake up, only reached the edge of consciousness and went back. The racket, however, instantly awakened my mother, in the next room, who came to the immediate conclusion that her worst dread was realized: the big wooden bed upstairs had fallen on father. She therefore screamed, "Let's go to your poor father!" It was this shout, rather than the noise of my cot falling, that awakened my brother Herman, in the same room with her. He thought that mother had become, for no apparent reason, hysterical. "You're all right, mamma!" he shouted, trying to calm her. They exchanged shout for shout for perhaps ten seconds: "Let's go to your poor father!" and "You're all right!" That woke up Briggs. By this time I was conscious of what was going on, in a vague way, but did not yet realize that I was under my bed instead of on it. Briggs, awakening in the midst of loud shouts of fear and apprehension, came to the quick conclusion that he was suffocating and that we were all trying to "bring him out." With a low moan, he grasped the glass of camphor at the head of his bed and instead of sniffing it poured it over himself. The room reeked of camphor. "Ugf, ahfg!" choked Briggs, like a drowning man, for he had almost succeeded in stopping his breath under the deluge of pungent spirits. He leaped out of bed and groped toward the open window, but came up against one that was closed. With his hand, he beat out the glass, and I could hear it crash and tinkle in the alleyway below. It was at this juncture that I, in trying to get up, had the uncanny sensation of feeling my bed above me! Foggy with sleep, I now suspected, in my turn, that the whole uproar was being made in a frantic endeavor to extricate me from what must be an unheard-of and perilous situation. "Get me out of this!" I bawled. "Get me out!" I think I had the nightmarish belief that I was entombed in a mine. "Gugh!" gasped Briggs, floundering in his camphor.

By this time my mother, still shouting, pursued by Herman, still shouting, was trying to open the door to the attic, in order to go up and get my father's body out of the wreckage. The door was stuck, however, and wouldn't yield. Her frantic pulls on it only added to the general banging and confusion. Roy and the dog were now up, one shouting questions, the other barking.

Father, farthest away and soundest sleeper of all, had by this time been awakened by the battering on the attic door. He decided that the house was on fire. "I'm coming, I'm coming!" he wailed in a slow, sleepy voice—it took him many minutes to regain full consciousness. My mother, still believing he was caught under the bed, detected in his "I'm coming!" the mournful, resigned note of one who is preparing to meet his Maker. "He's dying!" she shouted.

"I'm all right!" Briggs yelled, to reassure her. "I'm all right!" He still believed that it was his own closeness to death that was worrying mother. I found at last the light switch in my room, unlocked the door, and Briggs and I joined the others at the attic door. The dog, who never did like Briggs, jumped for him —assuming that he was the culprit in whatever was going on—and Roy had to throw Rex and hold him. We could hear father crawling out of bed upstairs. Roy pulled the attic door open, with a mighty jerk, and father came down the stairs, sleepy and irritable but safe and sound. My mother began to weep when she saw him. Rex began to howl. "What in the name of God is going on here?" asked father.

The situation was finally put together like a gigantic jigsaw puzzle. Father caught a cold from prowling around in his bare feet but there were no other bad results. "I'm glad," said mother, who always looked on the bright side of things, "that your grandfather wasn't here."

Father Opens
My Mail

Clarence Day

There was a time in my boyhood when I felt that Father had handicapped me severely in life by naming me after him, "Clarence." All literature, so far as I could see, was thronged with objectionable persons named Clarence. Percy was bad enough, but there had been some good fighters named Percy. The only Clarence in history was a duke who did something dirty at Tewkesbury, and who died a ridiculous death afterwards in a barrel of malmsey.

As for the Clarences in the fiction I read, they were horrible. In one story, for instance, there were two brothers, Clarence and Frank. Clarence was a "vain, disagreeable little fellow," who was proud of his curly hair and fine clothes, while Frank was a "rollicking boy who was ready to play games with anybody." Clarence didn't like to play games, of course. He just minced around looking on.

One day when the mother of these boys had gone out, this story went on, Clarence "tempted" Frank to disobey her and fly their kite on the roof. Frank didn't want to, but Clarence kept taunting him and daring him until Frank was stung into doing it. After the two boys went up to the roof, Frank got good and dirty, running up and down and stumbling over scuttles, while Clarence sat there, giving him orders, and kept his natty clothes tidy. To my horror, he even spread out his handkerchief on the trapdoor to sit on. And to crown all, this sneak told on Frank as soon as their mother came in.

This wasn't an exceptionally mean Clarence, either. He was just run-of-the-mill. Some were worse.

So far as I could ever learn, however, Father had never heard of these stories, and had never dreamed of there being anything objectionable in his name. Quite the contrary. And yet as a boy he had lived a good rough-and-tumble boy's life. He had played and fought on the city streets, and kept a dog in Grandpa's stable, and stolen rides to Greenpoint Ferry on the high, lurching bus. In the summer he had gone to West Springfield and had run down Shad Lane through the trees to the house where Grandpa was born, and had gone barefoot and driven the cows home just as though he had been named Tom or Bill.

He had the same character as a boy, I suppose, that he had as a man, and he was too independent to care if people thought his name fancy. He paid no attention to the prejudices of others, except to disapprove of them. He had plenty of prejudices himself, of course, but they were his own. He was humorous and confident and level-headed, and I imagine that if any boy had tried to make fun of him for being named Clarence, Father would simply have laughed and told him he didn't know what he was talking about.

I asked Mother how this name had ever happened to spring up in our family. She explained that my great-great-grandfather was Benjamin Day, and my great-grandfather was Henry, and consequently my grandfather had been named Benjamin Henry. He in turn had named his eldest son Henry and his second son Benjamin. The result was that when Father was born there was no family name left. The privilege of choosing a name for Father had thereupon been given to Grandma, and unluckily for the Day family she had been reading a novel, the hero of which was named Clarence.

I knew that Grandma, though very like Grandpa in some respects, had a dreamy side which he hadn't, a side that she usually kept to herself, in her serene, quiet way. Her romantic choice of this name probably made Grandpa smile, but he was a detached sort of man who didn't take small matters seriously, and who drew a good deal of private amusement from the happenings of everyday life. Besides, he was partly to blame in this case, because that novel was one he had published himself in his magazine.

I asked Mother, when she had finished, why I had been named Clarence too.

It hadn't been her choice, Mother said. She had suggested all sorts of names to Father, but there seemed to be something wrong with each one. When she had at last spoken of naming me after him, however, he had said at once that that was the best suggestion yet—he said it sounded just right.

Father and I would have had plenty of friction in any case. This identity of names made things worse. Every time that I had been more of a fool than he liked, Father would try to impress on me my responsibilities as his eldest son, and above all as the son to whom he had given his name, as he put it. A great deal was expected, it seemed to me, of a boy who was named after his father. I used to envy my brothers, who didn't have anything expected of them on this score at all.

I envied them still more after I was old enough to begin getting letters. I then discovered that when Father "gave" me his name he had also, not unnaturally, I had to admit, retained it himself, and when anything came for Clarence S. Day he opened it, though it was sometimes for me.

He also opened everything that came addressed to Clarence S. Day, Jr. He didn't do this intentionally, but unless the "Jr." was clearly written, it looked like "Esq.," and anyhow Father was too accustomed to open all Clarence Day letters to remember about looking carefully every time for a "Jr." So far as mail and express went, I had no name at all of my own.

For the most part nobody wrote to me when I was a small boy except firms whose advertisements I had read in the *Youth's Companion* and to whom I had written requesting them to send me their circulars. These circulars described remarkable bargains in magicians' card outfits, stamps and coins, pocket knives, trick spiders, and imitation fried eggs, and they seemed interesting and valuable to me when I got them. The trouble was that Father usually got them and at once tore them up. I then had to write for such circulars again, and if Father got the second one too, he would sometimes explode with annoyance. He became particularly indignant one year, I remember, when he was repeatedly urged to take advantage of a special bargain sale of false whiskers. He said that he couldn't understand why these offerings kept pouring in. I knew why, in this case, but at other times I was often surprised myself at the number he got, not realizing that as a result of my postcard request my or our name had been automatically put on several large general mailing lists.

During this period I got more of my mail out of Father's wastebasket than I did from the postman.

At the age of twelve or thirteen, I stopped writing for these childish things and turned to a new field. Father and I, whichever of us got at the mail first, then began to receive not merely circulars but personal letters beginning:

DEAR FRIEND DAY:

In reply to your valued request for one of our Mammoth Agents' Outfits, kindly forward postoffice order for $1.49 to cover cost of postage and packing, and we will put you in a position to earn a large income in your spare time with absolutely no labor on your part, by taking subscriptions for *The Secret Handbook of Mesmerism,* and our *Tales of Blood* series.

And one spring, I remember, as the result of what I had intended to be a secret application on my part, Father was assigned "the exclusive rights for Staten Island and Hoboken of selling the Gem Home Popper for Pop Corn. Housewives buy it at sight."

After Father had stormily endured these afflictions for a while, he and I began to get letters from girls. Fortunately for our feelings, these were rare, but they were ordeals for both of us. Father had forgotten, if he ever knew, how silly young girls can sound, and I got my first lesson in how unsystematic they were. No matter how private and playful they meant their letters to be, they forgot to put "Jr." on the envelope every once in so often. When Father opened these letters, he read them all the way through, sometimes twice, muttering to himself over and over: "This is very peculiar. I don't understand this at all. Here's a letter to me from some person I never heard of. I can't see what it's about." By the time it had occurred to him that possibly the letter might be for me, I was red and embarrassed and even angrier at the girl than at Father. And on days when he had read some of the phrases aloud to the family, it nearly killed me to claim it.

Lots of fellows whom I knew had been named after their fathers without having such troubles. But although Father couldn't have been kinder-hearted or had any better intentions, when he saw his name on a package or envelope it never dawned on him that it might not be for him. He was too active in his habits to wait until I had a chance to get at it. And as he was also single-minded and prompt to attend to unfinished business, he opened everything automatically and then did his best to dispose of it.

This went on even after I grew up, until I had a home of my own. Father was always perfectly decent about it, but he never changed. When he saw I felt sulky, he was genuinely sorry and said so, but he couldn't see why all this should annoy me, and he was surprised and amused that it did. I used to get angry once in a while when something came for me which I particularly hadn't wished him to see and which I would find lying, opened, on the hall table marked "For Jr.?" when I came in; but nobody could stay angry with Father—he was too utterly guiltless of having meant to offend.

He often got angry himself, but it was mostly at

things, not at persons, and he didn't mind a bit (as a rule) when persons got angry at him. He even declared, when I got back from college, feeling dignified, and told him that I wished he'd be more careful, that he suffered from these mistakes more than I did. It wasn't *his* fault, he pointed out, if my stupid correspondents couldn't remember my name, and it wasn't any pleasure to him to be upset at his breakfast by finding that a damned lunatic company in Battle Creek had sent him a box of dry bread crumbs, with a letter asserting that this rubbish would be good for his stomach. "I admit I threw it into the fireplace, Clarence, but what else could I do? If you valued this preposterous concoction, my dear boy, I'm sorry. I'll buy another box for you today, if you'll tell me where I can get it. Don't feel badly! I'll buy you a barrel. Only I hope you won't eat it."

In the days when Mrs. Pankhurst and her friends were chaining themselves to lamp-posts in London, in their campaign for the vote, a letter came from Frances Hand trustfully asking "Dear Clarence" to do something to help Woman Suffrage—speak at a meeting, I think. Father got red in the face. "Speak at one of their meetings!" he roared at Mother. "I'd like nothing better! You can tell Mrs. Hand that it would give me great pleasure to inform all those crackpots in petticoats exactly what I think of their antics."

"Now, Clare," Mother said, "you mustn't talk that way. I like that nice Mrs. Hand, and anyhow this letter must be for Clarence."

One time I asked Father for his opinion of a low-priced stock I'd been watching. His opinion was that it was not worth a damn. I thought this over, but I still wished to buy it, so I placed a scale order with another firm instead of with Father's office, and said nothing about it. At the end of the month this other firm sent me a statement, setting forth each of my little transactions in full, and of course they forgot to put the "Jr." at the end of my name. When Father opened the envelope, he thought at first in his excitement that this firm had actually opened an account for him without being asked. I found him telling Mother that he'd like to wring their damned necks.

"That must be for me, Father," I said, when I took in what had happened.

We looked at each other.

"You bought this stuff?" he said incredulously. "After all I said about it?"

"Yes, Father."

He handed over the statement and walked out of the room.

Both he and I felt offended and angry. We stayed so for several days, too, but we then made it up.

Once in a while when I got a letter that I had no time to answer I used to address an envelope to the sender and then put anything in it that happened to be lying around on my desk—a circular about books, a piece of newspaper, an old laundry bill—anything at all, just to be amiable, and yet at the same time to save myself the trouble of writing. I happened to tell several people about this private habit of mine at a dinner one night—a dinner at which Alice Duer Miller and one or two other writers were present. A little later she wrote me a criticism of Henry James and ended by saying that I needn't send her any of my old laundry bills because she wouldn't stand it. And she forgot to put on the "Jr."

"In the name of God," Father said bleakly, "this is the worst yet. Here's a woman who says I'd better not read *The Golden Bowl*, which I have no intention whatever of doing, and she also warns me for some unknown reason not to send her my laundry bills."

The good part of all these experiences, as I realize now, was that in the end they drew Father and me closer together. My brothers had only chance battles with him. I had a war. Neither he nor I relished its clashes, but they made us surprisingly intimate.

Pencil-Chewing

Frank Sullivan

The pencil-chewers constitute one class of unfortunates whose misery science has done nothing to relieve. These poor creatures cannot see a pencil lying about loose without being seized by a craving to make a meal of it. They are on the increase, and something ought to be done, not only for their sakes but in the interest of forest conservation. With the Japanese beetle destroying the elms and the Christmas-tree brokers hacking away at the firs, the timber situation in the United States is bad enough without having people eating cedar unnecessarily.

You see traces of the pencil-chewers everywhere. I am writing this very protest in a fit of pique because a moment ago I picked up a chewed pencil. It looked as though it had been worried by a neurotic beaver. It had been gnawed with an avidity that bordered on the dendrophilic. Most pencil-eaters content themselves with nibbling at the unsharpened end of the pencil, then passing on to other pencils, like tapirs ravishing buds in a jungle. But this pencil has been permanently crippled.

Obviously, the addict who wrought this havoc was in an advanced stage of the habit, and probably incurable. In such a case the only humane thing to do is to feed the poor creature all the pencils he can eat, so that me may succumb to lead and cedar poisoning as quickly as possible, to find peace in a perhaps pencil-less Beyond.

It has never ceased to be a source of wonderment to me why a man should prefer to chew pencils when food that is far more wholesome and filling can be procured at a trifling cost. No pencil-chewer can tell me he cannot afford better food. A bowl of good nourishing soup can be had anywhere for the price of a soft lead pencil, and contains more calories. Anyhow, persons who are really hungry are rarely pencil-chewers. The latter are recruited from the better-fed but more hysterical upper classes. They claim that chewing on a pencil helps them to think. There was a case here in New York last fall of a prominent American novelist who, during the writing of one of these eleven-hundred-page novels that are all the rage now, swallowed so much cedar that he had to go to the hospital shortly before Christmas to be operated on, and they removed enough timber from him to supply the Yule log for the Christmas celebration at the hospital. He sent the hospital a bill for three dollars for wood and supplies.

Sometimes pencil-chewers can go for years and years without giving any outward indications of the habit, such as sprouting cedar twigs or having pine knots appear on their elbows, but eventually it gets them. An addict I heard of gnawed pencils for thirty years without seeming to suffer any ill effects, until one day, to everybody's surprise, he suddenly screamed that he was a pencil and tried to stick his head into the office pencil-sharpener. Rescued from the sharpener, he kept trying to nestle in his stenographer's ear. He recovered eventually, but not until he had gone about for a long time begging his friends to whittle him.

What can we do to help the pencil-gnawer? It is no use suggesting a Stop Selling These campaign to limit the sale of pencils to proved non-chewers. This would only increase pencil-chewing by making it more alluring.

It might be possible to help the chewer by diverting his attention to more succulent tidbits. Let him make it a rule never to approach a pencil when hungry; never to use a pencil on an empty stomach. That will lessen the urge to eat the pencil. Then, while using a pencil, let the addict arrange to have a supply of food close at hand. The food ought to be tempting, so as to outweigh the charms of the pencil—a tasty custard, a bonbon, a spiced cookie, or a forkful of finnan haddie. Then, whenever he feels the urge to take a bite of the pencil, he can reach for one of the more orthodox dainties.

Or we can attack the problem from another angle. We can make it impossible for the addict to chew the pencil by making a pencil that is impossible to chew. The trouble with present pencils is that they are made of soft woods, easy to chew. The unchewable pencil would be made of teak, which is one of the hardest woods in the world, comes from Ceylon and has never been successfully gnawed. A teak pencil would be apt to thwart the efforts of the most determined pencil-nibbler, and save him from himself. Care should be taken, however, least the nibbler, in a fit of rage at finding himself baffled, swallow the pencil entire.

In the last analysis, the most thorough method of

dealing with the problem of pencil-chewing is through education. Pencil-chewers become pencil-chewers because chewing pencils helps them to think. Therefore, it is the task of those who wish to help them to train them in the use of other, and less harmful, aids to thought.

There are many such aids. Lots of thinkers who never touch a pencil get excellent results by tearing their hair and rolling their eyes frantically, as a stimulant to the production of creative work. This, however, does not mean that a thinker who is bald, or who cannot roll his eyes, or both, must resort to chewing pencils. Not at all. There are still other aids to thought.

Biting the lower lip, for instance, is one of the best. Many of our foremost pundits do their most effective thinking while biting the lower lip. This method accomplishes fully as much to help speed the thought process as biting on a lead pencil, and is neater and not nearly so dangerous. Neater, because thinkers cannot leave old bitten lips around on desks for other thinkers to pick up; less dangerous, because the lower lip can stand a good deal of biting without suffering any material damage. If occasionally, in the course of some particularly brilliant job of thinking, a wiseacre absent-mindedly nips off a portion of his lip, the damage is soon remedied by Mother Nature, or by surgery.

If you are a bald thinker, and you cannot or do not care to roll your eyes, and are averse to biting the lower lip, you can groan or mumble, or wring the hands, as an aid to creative output. Personally, I am a groaner and an eye-roller, with intervals of mumbling and wringing the hands. I also chew a pencil occasionally, but in moderation. All during this article, for instance, I have been mumbling and uttering low screams, rolling the right eye appealingly toward heaven from time to time. Perhaps you have, too.

Who's on First?

Abbott and Costello

Variety Act

ABBOTT: You know, strange as it may seem, they give ballplayers nowadays very peculiar names . . . Now, on the St. Louis team Who's on first, What's on second, I Don't Know is on third—

COSTELLO: That's what I want to find out. I want you to tell me the names of the fellows on the St. Louis team.

ABBOTT: I'm telling you. Who's on first, What's on second, I Don't Know is on third—

COSTELLO: You know the fellows' names?

ABBOTT: Yes.

COSTELLO: Well, then who's playing first?

ABBOTT: Yes.

COSTELLO: I mean the fellow's name on first base.

ABBOTT: Who.

COSTELLO: The fellow playin' first base.

ABBOTT: Who.

COSTELLO: The guy on first base.

ABBOTT: Who is on first.

COSTELLO: Well, what are you askin' me for?

ABBOTT: I'm not asking you—I'm telling you. Who is on first.

COSTELLO: I'm asking you—who's on first?

ABBOTT: That's the man's name!

COSTELLO: That's who's name?

ABBOTT: Yes.

COSTELLO: Well, go ahead tell me!

ABBOTT: Who.

COSTELLO: Have you got a first baseman on first?

ABBOTT: Certainly.

COSTELLO: Then who's playing first?

ABBOTT: Absolutely.

COSTELLO: Well, all I'm trying to find out is what's the guy's name on first base.

ABBOTT: Oh, no, no. What is on second base.

COSTELLO: I'm not asking you who's on second.

ABBOTT: Who's on first.

COSTELLO: That's what I'm trying to find out.

ABBOTT: Now, take it easy.

COSTELLO: What's the guy's name on first base?

ABBOTT: What's the guy's name on second base.

COSTELLO: I'm not askin' ya who's on second.

ABBOTT: Who's on first.

COSTELLO: I don't know.

ABBOTT: He's on third.

COSTELLO: If I mentioned the third baseman's name, who did I say is playing third?

ABBOTT: No, Who's playing first.

COSTELLO: Stay offa first, will ya?

ABBOTT: Well, what do you want me to do?

COSTELLO: Now, what's the guy's name on first base?

ABBOTT: What's on second.

COSTELLO: I'm not asking ya who's on second.

ABBOTT: Who's on first.

COSTELLO: I don't know.

ABBOTT: He's on third.

COSTELLO: There I go back to third again.

ABBOTT: Please. Now what is it you want to know?

COSTELLO: What is the fellow's name on third base?

ABBOTT: What is the fellow's name on second base.

COSTELLO: I'm not askin' ya who's on second.

ABBOTT: Who's on first.

COSTELLO: I don't know. *(Makes noise)* You got an outfield?

ABBOTT: Oh, sure.

COSTELLO: The left fielder's name?

ABBOTT: Why.

COSTELLO: I just thought I'd ask.

ABBOTT: Well, I just thought I'd tell you.

COSTELLO: Then tell me who's playing left field.

ABBOTT: Who's playing first.

COSTELLO: Stay out of the infield. I want to know
           what's the fellow's name in left field.

ABBOTT: What is on second.

COSTELLO: I'm not asking you who's on second.

ABBOTT: Now take it easy, take it easy.

COSTELLO: And the left fielder's name?

ABBOTT: Why.

COSTELLO: Because.

ABBOTT: Oh, he's center field.

COSTELLO: Wait a minute. You got a pitcher?

ABBOTT: Wouldn't this be a fine team without a
           pitcher?

COSTELLO: Tell me the pitcher's name.

ABBOTT: Tomorrow.

COSTELLO: You don't want to tell me today?

ABBOTT: I'm telling you, man.

COSTELLO: Then go ahead.

ABBOTT: Tomorrow.

COSTELLO: What time tomorrow are you gonna tell me who's pitching?

ABBOTT: Now listen. Who is not pitching. Who is on—

COSTELLO: I'll break your arm if you say who's on first.

ABBOTT: Then why come up here and ask?

COSTELLO: I want to know what's the pitcher's name.

ABBOTT: What's on second.

COSTELLO: Ya gotta catcher?

ABBOTT: Yes.

COSTELLO: The catcher's name?

ABBOTT: Today.

COSTELLO: Today. And Tomorrow's pitching.

ABBOTT: Yes.

COSTELLO: I'm a good catcher too, you know.

ABBOTT: I know that.

COSTELLO: I would like to catch. Tomorrow's pitching and I'm catching.

ABBOTT: Yes.

COSTELLO: Tomorrow throws the ball and the guy up bunts the ball.

ABBOTT: Yes.

COSTELLO: Now when he bunts the ball—me being a good catcher—I want to throw the guy out at first base, so I pick up the ball and throw it to who?

ABBOTT: Now, that's the first thing you've said right.

COSTELLO: I DON'T EVEN KNOW WHAT I'M TALKING ABOUT.

ABBOTT: Well, that's all you have to do.

COSTELLO: Is to throw it to first base.

ABBOTT: Yes.

COSTELLO: Now who's got it?

ABBOTT: Naturally.

COSTELLO: Who has it?

ABBOTT: Naturally.

COSTELLO: O.K.

ABBOTT: Now you've got it.

COSTELLO: I pick up the ball and I throw it to Naturally.

ABBOTT: No you don't. You throw the ball to first base.

COSTELLO: Then who gets it?

ABBOTT: Naturally.

COSTELLO: I throw the ball to Naturally.

ABBOTT: You don't. You throw it to Who.

COSTELLO: Naturally.

ABBOTT: Well, naturally. Say it that way.

COSTELLO: I said I'd throw the ball to Naturally.

ABBOTT: You don't. You throw it to Who.

COSTELLO: Naturally.

ABBOTT: Yes.

COSTELLO: So I throw the ball to first base and Naturally gets it.

ABBOTT: No. You throw the ball to first base—

COSTELLO: Then who gets it?

ABBOTT: Naturally.

COSTELLO: That's what I'm saying.

ABBOTT: You're not saying that.

COSTELLO: I throw the ball to first base.

ABBOTT: Then Who gets it.

COSTELLO: He better get it.

ABBOTT: That's it. All right now, don't get excited. Take it easy.

COSTELLO: Now I throw the ball to first base, whoever it is grabs the ball, so the guy runs to second.

ABBOTT: Uh-Huh.

COSTELLO: Who picks up the ball and throws it to what. What throws it to I Don't Know. I Don't Know throws it back to tomorrow—a triple play.

ABBOTT: Yeah. It could be.

COSTELLO: Another guy gets up and it's a long fly
             ball to center. Why? I don't know. And I
             don't care.

ABBOTT: What was that?

COSTELLO: I said, I don't care.

ABBOTT: Oh, that's our shortstop.

COSTELLO: *(Makes noises—steps close to Abbott and they
             glare at each other)*

She Was Only Jokes

She was only a telephone operator's daughter, but she had good connections!

a blacksmith's daughter, but she knew how to forge ahead.

a milkman's daughter, but she was the cream of the crop.

a waitress's daughter, but she sure could dish it out.

a quarryman's daughter, but she took everything for granite.

an electrician's daughter, but she went haywire.

a moonshiner's daughter, but I love her still.

an artist's daughter, but she knew where to draw the line.

a plumber's daughter, but she was an awful drip.

a fruit store owner's daughter, but oh what a peach.

a poet's daughter, but I've seen verse.

a doctor's daughter, but she knew how to operate.

6.

1940-1949

American Humor Fights Back

Cartoon—Bill Mauldin
Fibber McGee and Molly
The Wonderful Adventures of Paul Bunyan—Louis
    Untermeyer
Charles—Shirley Jackson
Little Moron Jokes

Introduction

The United States was involved in World War II for five years. During this period comic writers and performers at home and overseas exploited the lighter side of the war effort in an attempt to bolster the spirits of soldiers and the nation at large. This was also an expression of the American characteristic of joking in time of danger or discomfort.

A very special kind of humor is present among troops in wartime, whether they are under attack on the battlefield or enduring the deadly tedium and depersonalization stemming from living cheek by jowl with fellow soldiers. "Barrack-room humor" is aptly named. One of the foremost exponents of this kind of comedy was Bill Mauldin, soldier-illustrator of the familiar figure of G. I. Joe, which appeared in "Stars and Stripes" and elsewhere.

On the home front the professional comedians made fun of rationing, of the black marketeer, of the inconveniences of price control. There was a darker side to humor also that reflected people's confusion over the destruction of war, their terror when trying to understand the atom bomb. And as Americans were becoming more sophisticated about international affairs, this too showed up in the humor of the day.

"Now that ya mention it, it does sound like th' patter of rain on a tin roof."

Fibber McGee and Molly

Radio Show Script

FIBBER: Gotta straighten out that closet one of these days, Molly. I don't see that electric cord any place. I must have put it someplace where—Oh my gosh!

MOLLY: Now what?

FIBBER: Look! My old mandolin—remember?

MOLLY: Well, what are you getting so misty eyed about it now for? It falls out of the closet every time you open it.

FIBBER: It always falls outa the closet but this is the first time the case has busted open. My gosh—my old mandolin! Needs a little tuning, I guess.

MOLLY: A little tuning! That's about as melodious as a slate pencil!

FIBBER: I sure used to be a wiz on this thing. Remember how we used to go canoeing on the Illinois River and I used to serenade you with my old mandolin?

MOLLY: I never knew whether you took up the mandolin because you loved music or hated paddling.

FIBBER: And remember the time you dropped the paddle to applaud one of my songs and we had to paddle home with the mandolin?

MOLLY: I wasn't applauding. I was swatting mosquitoes.

FIBBER: Sounded like applauding. Ahhh, my old mandolin! Wonder what would be the best thing to polish it up with?

MOLLY: If you don't know that, dearie, you'd better really learn to play that thing, or take a course in scissors grinding.

FIBBER: Let's see now—how did "Redwing" go? Ohhh—moon shines tonight on pretty Redwing—the breezes sighing—the nightshirts—the nightmares—the night—

MOLLY: Night birds.

FIBBER: Oh, yes, the nightbirds crying—

MOLLY: Oh, hello, Alice.

ALICE: Hello, Mrs. McGee. Creepers, Mr. McGee—what made that ping-pong paddle swell all up like that?

FIBBER: This, my dear girl, is not a ping-pong paddle. This is my old mandolin. I guess the love of good music is just something that's gotta be born into a person. They probably sneered at Rachmaninoff too, when he first took up the violin.

ALICE: They probably did. He played the piano.

FIBBER: Did I say Rachmaninoff? I meant Benny Goodman.

MOLLY: He plays the clarinet.

ALICE: But we know what you mean, Mr. McGee. Can you really play that mandolin?

FIBBER: Can I play it? I may be a little outa practice, Alice, but I can still dash off a snappy little arpeggio or two. Want me to sing something for you? Like maybe—"Pretty Redwing"?

ALICE: What's it from?

FIBBER: Ohhh, I dunno about that! Mark my words, it'll be popular again. I'll never forget the time I first learned to play "Pretty Redwing" all the way through. I was so happy I played it all day.

ALICE: How does it go, Mr. McGee?

FIBBER: Like this—Oh, the moon shines tonight on pretty Redwing . . .

MOLLY: Wasn't that good, Alice? Did you get that Th-r-r-r-rummmm in the middle of it? And he's only using two hands.

FIBBER: I gotta brush up a bit, Alice. My gosh, I haven't seen my old mandolin for fifteen years.

ALICE: Is it a pretty difficult instrument?

MOLLY: To play or ignore?

FIBBER: It is pretty tough, Alice. It ain't like a

Hawaiian steel guitar, where you can start any place and sneak up on a note.

MOLLY: Well, heavenly days—Doctor Gamble.

DOCTOR
GAMBLE: Hello, Molly. Hello, Neanderthal.

FIBBER: Hyah, Arrowsmith. Kick your case of corn cures into a corner and compose your corpulent corpus on a convenient camp chair.

DOCTOR
GAMBLE: Thanks, McGee. Your hospitality is equalled only by your personal beauty. And the prosecution rests.

MOLLY: Had a lot of operations, Doctor? You look tired.

DOCTOR
GAMBLE: My dear, I've had more people in stitches today than Bob Hope. But tell me, what's our one-string fiddler doing with the potbellied Stradivarius?

FIBBER: This, my ignorant bonebender, is a mandolin. My old mandolin. Just found it again after all these years.

MOLLY: I just love mandolin music, don't you, Doctor?

DOCTOR
GAMBLE: I used to, but my love soon ripened into disgust. If you really get good with that snycopating cigar box, McGee, and want to

run away and join the gypsies, I'll be glad to pierce your ears for earrings.

FIBBER: Doc, what you know about music, you could stand across the room and toss thru the eye of a needle. Listen to this—(*Plucks the string*) Is that a beautiful tone, or isn't it?

DOCTOR
GAMBLE: Frankly, sonny, it's brutal.

MOLLY: Well, he's a little out of practice, Doctor. Heavenly days, he hasn't touched the mandolin for fifteen or twenty years.

DOCTOR
GAMBLE: Let's count it among our blessings.

FIBBER: Oh, don't be so cynical, you narry minded old muscle-meddler. Lemme play something for you.

MOLLY: What do you want him to play for you, Doctor?

DOCTOR
GAMBLE: Nine holes of golf, and don't hurry back.

FIBBER: He's just a hardshell, Molly. But I can break him into little quivering pieces with some simple old folksong—one of those heartwarming melodies that are so close to the soul and spirit of our national entity. The natural rhythm of a new frontier, throbbing with the pulsing energy of a dynamic destiny.

DOCTOR
GAMBLE: What's he talking about?

MOLLY: "Pretty Redwing." Play it for the Doctor, McGee.

FIBBER: Okay. You wanna hear "Pretty Redwing," Doc? Or rather I play something else?

DOCTOR
GAMBLE: What else can you play?

MOLLY: "The Moon Shines Tonight."

DOCTOR
GAMBLE: That's better. Play that, McGee.
(*McGee plays tune*)

DOCTOR
GAMBLE: McGee, I don't like to be hypercritical, but I've heard prettier music than that from a beer truck running over a manhole cover.

FIBBER: Oh yeah? And when did you become a music critic, you big fat epidemic chaser?

DOCTOR
GAMBLE: Why, you uncultured little faker, I've got more music in the first phalanx of my left pinkie than you have in your entire family tree!

FIBBER: Don't call me a phalanx, you soggy, sap-headed serum salesman! Any time I want any advice from you, I'll ask for it.

DOCTOR
GAMBLE: If there wasn't a lady present, I'd give you

some right now, you posturing little—don't threaten me with that mandolin!!

FIBBER: I'll bust it over your thick skull so hard . . .

MOLLY: McGee!

FIBBER: Eh?

MOLLY: Behave yourself. You too, Doctor. You're acting like children.

DOCTOR
GAMBLE: I'm sorry. Certainly is a beautiful instrument you got there, McGee. Needs tuning though.

FIBBER: It does? How do you know?

DOCTOR
GAMBLE: I can hear it. Here, let me tune it for you.

FIBBER: Okay
(*Doc tunes mandolin*)

DOCTOR
GAMBLE: Now, let's see how it sounds. (*Plays a fancy selection*)

MOLLY: My word!

FIBBER: My Gosh!

DOCTOR
GAMBLE: My hat. Good day.
(*Door slams*)

FIBBER: Ohhh, that burns me up—that really burns me up.

MOLLY: Well now, don't you feel badly, dearie. I'll

bet Doctor Gamble studied a lot longer than you did. You just stay with it. You'll get it.

FIBBER: Well, I'm glad there's one person around here who ain't trying' to show me up for a chump. Even if you could play this thing, you wouldn't do it.

MOLLY: I certainly won't.

FIBBER: Whaddye mean you won't?

MOLLY: I mean no matter how my fingers itch for a mandolin again, I'll restrain myself.

FIBBER: You mean . . . you . . . you used to play one of these?

MOLLY: Only in high school, McGee, and then only simple little pieces like this—here—let me take it.

FIBBER: Okay.

(Molly plays "Redwing" skillfully.)

FIBBER: Oh, this is really ridiculous!

The Wonderful Adventures of Paul Bunyan

Louis Untermeyer

The blue snow continued to fall. It spread over
Michigan and Minnesota; it stretched across the whole
Northwest.

"There must be an end to it," said Paul to Johnny
Inkslinger, early one ice-blue morning. "I'm going to
do some exploring. Tell the men to go on with their
work—they've got plenty of food now—and I'll be
back with good news, or I won't be back at all."

So Paul tramped out of the woods, cleared a few
rivers, strode across a mountain or two; and there he
was on the shores of Lake Superior, greatest of the
Great Lakes. Ice-cakes were tossing on freezing waves,
booming against each other, thudding and splintering.
It sounded as if all the timber in the world were crashing upon the echoing shore.

One huge wave of white water lifted itself above the
others; and there, among the grinding ice-cakes, Paul
saw two ears. Nothing of the rest of the creature was
visible, nothing to show if it were man or monster
—just two huge ears. Then they disappeared.

Paul pulled his boots up to his hips and plunged
into the icy waters. The waves roared, the ice-cakes
heaved and boomed; but there was no sign of life in the
vast lake. Just as he was about to turn back, the two

ears appeared again. Paul threshed out and caught hold of them. He dragged them toward the shore and, as he pulled them out of the water, a head came into view, then a pair of shoulders, then two forelegs, a spindling body, rear legs, and an unhappy watersoaked tail. It was less than half alive, and all of it was sky-blue.

"Well," said Paul, carrying the little creature to his campfire on the shore, "if there can be blue snow, I suppose there can be a blue calf. Or maybe it's just blue with the cold."

But when Paul worked over it and rubbed its joints and warmed it in front of the fire, the calf did not change color. If anything, the color deepened, a brighter, healthier blue. Paul had a flask of buffalo milk with him, and he poured some of this down the calf's throat. The animal didn't open its eyes, but it gave the first sign of life. It shivered a little, and, as Paul bent over, licked his face.

"What a baby," laughed Paul. "I wonder if it thinks I'm its father or its mother. Anyway, a baby it is. And, if it lives, that's what I'll call it: Babe—Babe, the Blue Ox." And he wrapped a blanket around its little frame.

In the morning Babe's eyes were open and his tongue was hanging out.

"Looks as if it might be hungry—and there's no milk left. I don't suppose it will touch my hotcakes and coffee; and now that it's living, it will be a shame if it starves to death."

But Babe ate up the hotcakes, drank the coffee, and, still hungry, took a big bite out of the coffee-pot.

"You're quite a calf!" chuckled Paul, "you'll be quite a companion when you get your strength."

As though in answer, Babe struggled to his feet,

lowered his head, and butted Paul from the rear. Whether it was the blow itself or the shock of surprise, Paul was thrown ten feet and came down like a ton of rock.

"You're a little wonder," he laughed, getting to his feet and rubbing the snow out of his eyes. "You're the Babe for me. But I don't dare take you back to camp—not quite yet."

So he began feeding Babe. He tried him on every kind of food he could find—and at the end of every meal, Babe was always hungry. One day after Babe had lapped up six gallons of moose-moss soup, Paul went out to rustle up something for himself. When he returned, Babe had eaten the blankets and was chewing what was left of the pots and pans.

"Babe!" exclaimed Paul, half angry and half amused.

Babe tried to look guilty; he wanted to win Paul's sympathy with a weak and plaintive moo. But what came out of Babe was a monstrous roar, a bellow that shook the hills and knocked against the sky.

"That settles it," said Paul. "We're wasting time. If you're big enough to bellow, you're big enough to work. Now let's see if you can get to camp under your own power.

So they set out. It seemed to Paul that the further they walked, the bigger Babe grew. As he watched the young ox snort and stamp the ground, he could see the head take on weight and character, the chest grow deep and solid, the legs grow stocky, and the whole body toughen with force and energy.

When they reached camp, Babe was a match for Paul. He stood, as though sculptured out of blue stone, a giant among giants. The men were too flabbergasted to say anything. Johnny Inkslinger was the first to measure him.

"Forty-two axe-handles between the eyes—*and* a tobacco box," cried Johnny. "But there's no telling how much he weighs. There aren't scales strong enough."

"But what are you going to do with him?" asked Little Meery.

"Do? Just you wait and see," said Paul. "Just wait until he gets his growth."

Babe was full-grown by the end of the winter. The last of the blue snow melted, but Babe was bluer than ever—bluer and bigger. It was said that Babe was so long in the body you could never see all of him at one time, that Paul had to carry a pair of field glasses so he could see what the Blue Ox was doing with his hind feet. But that's probably an exaggeration. Paul knew what to do with Babe all right; and, for all his size, Babe followed Paul around like a puppy.

Even before Paul had Babe, he had his own way of logging. There never was a logger like Paul, not since acorns first learned to grow up into oaks. Squared timbers were his specialty. He'd pick out a tree. Then he'd give it four cuts—north, south, east, and west—four sharp slices from top to bottom on each side. Then, he would shout, "Timber-r-r!" so everyone would get out of the way. And when he had them all standing square and clean and shiny white, Paul would swing his axe from his waist just as if it were a scythe and he were mowing in a hayfield. Down the trees would come —Paul mowed those timbers an acre at a time—and then they were ready to be taken to market.

Getting them stacked and sorted and ready for

shipment was the hardest part of the work. But now that Paul had Babe, it was easy. The Galloping Kid would swing his lasso around the trees and pile up a couple of acres of timber just like cordwood. Then Paul would hitch Babe to the load, and Babe would drag the trees down to the lake—an acre of them at a time—and tip them over into the water, a huge raft of logs.

It was a pretty sight to see. The log-raft floating away, Paul singing and Babe pawing the ground. The big blue water and the white logs flashing by in the sunshine. And there was the smell of the pine and balsam sweetening the air. And there were the sounds of the forest far off—the scolding of a squirrel, the call of a thrush, and the axes biting into the clean wood.

There was no job too hard for Babe. He could haul anything anywhere. Whenever Paul decided to move to better logging grounds, the whole camp would be hitched to Babe; and the Blue Ox would take a deep breath, heave his mighty flanks, and drag the bunk-house, the kitchen, the dairy, and all the other houses behind him.

Perhaps Babe's hardest task was working on the narrow roads in upper Michigan. It wasn't so much the narrowness as the crookedness. Some of the roads were so crooked that they doubled back on each other, and the men would meet themselves coming back from work. But Paul fixed that. He attached one end of a cable to Babe, and the other end to the crooked road. Then he'd yell, "Pull, Babe—pul-l-l-l!"

And by the end of the winter Babe had straightened out every crooked road in northern Michigan.

But Babe had his troubles, too. He was always hungry; nothing could satisfy his appetite. Before Paul got his own hay farm, it used to take the teamsters six months to bring in one day's feed for the Blue Ox.

So Paul laid out a farm halfway between the camp and the lake—rich black loam laced by trout streams and refreshed, even on the hottest summer day, by underground springs. Since he wasn't a farmer, Paul hired a fellow from Vermont, Phil Plenty, to run the farm.

Phil Plenty was as good as his name. In Vermont they had only two seasons: winter and August. The fields were so rocky that Phil had to blast the boulders so he could plant potatoes; the cold was so intense that, six months out of twelve, the hens laid hard-boiled eggs. But now Phil had the kind of land every farmer dreams about—soil smooth as buckwheat honey, just enough clay to hold, just enough sand for drainage, warm enough for beans, cool enough for peas, not a stone in an acre, fertilized by centuries of minerals and leaf mould—a grower's paradise. Never did a farm yield so abundantly. The tomatoes grew as big as pumpkins; and the pumpkins were so big that, after he had scraped out the meat for pumpkin pies, Hot Biscuit Slim used the pumpkin shells instead of stalls for the young calves. The cabbages grew so large that two men had to saw the stalks before they could bring them in. As for the root vegetables—carrots, beets, parsnips, and turnips—the men could never get to the bottom of them; they kept on breaking them off no matter how deep they dug with their spades, until finally Paul had to invent the steam shovel to get them out of the ground. And the bees! Paul had sent east for a couple of hives so that the men could have honey with their biscuits. and the bees fattened on the giant wildflowers to such an extent that they became the size of eagles.

Babe loved the farm products and—with a few tons of hay as a snack between meals—he thrived on them all. But there was one particular vegetable he loved more than any other: parsnips—and his greed for parsnips was almost the death of him.

Phil Plenty had begun by being fond of Babe. But Babe's appetite was so enormous that Phil couldn't raise things fast enough—Babe was always a crop ahead of him. Phil and his farmers ploughed and fertilized and harrowed and cultivated and weeded and worked the fields—but Babe was always waiting to be fed. A bushel of beans topped off with a wheelbarrow-load of cabbages was just a comfortable cud for the Blue Ox. When Paul's loggers complained they weren't getting enough farmstuff, Phil took it to heart. He worked his men harder; but the more things they grew, the more Babe ate. It made Phil bitter.

"That blue monster! All our work for nothing! He'll eat us out of house and home and off the earth! If there were only some way of getting rid of him!"

Phil thought of many plans. But they came to nothing. He dreamed of starving the creature, of going on strike and refusing to raise another vegetable, of an earthquake that would bury Babe or a mighty hurricane that would carry him off. But next morning Babe would be there, bellowing louder than ever for his daily rations. And back to the fields Phil would go with a heavy heart and dark thoughts.

Paul seldom visited the farm, so Phil Plenty was startled when Paul's long shadow fell across the cornfield one evening. "We're moving camp for a while," said Paul. "So you'll have to ship the crops to Wisconsin; I'll leave a few hundred horse teams to carry the stuff over. I'll want lots of fodder and all the fancy extras—especially the bee-hives with the honey. And don't forget Babe. It'll be tough work, and Babe will want plenty of his favorite parsnips."

Parsnips! That gave Phil his great idea. He knew that if he let the first growth of parsnips go to seed, the second growth would come up poison. And it was the second growth that Phil planned to ship to the Wisconsin camp.

"And that," chuckled Phil, "will be the end of that oversized bully, that blighted and bloated old Blue Ox!"

So Phil worked as he had never worked before. He lengthened the working day; he drove his men eighteen hours out of twenty-four; he enlarged the parsnip fields; he raised the greatest crop of second growth parsnips—poison parsnips—ever attempted. At last it was finished. It took two whole weeks just to load the crop, and one cool morning before dawn, horse teams brought the first of the parsnips into the Wisconsin camp.

Babe was just awake. He sniffed the air. He recognized the odor of his favorite delicacy. He pawed the ground, gave a happy snort, and started for the pile.

But Little Meery was ahead of him. Little Meery had always suspected Phil Plenty. He had heard the farmer muttering about Babe, and once he had heard him tell his men that he had a plan to make their work easier for them. Besides, Little Meery didn't like the color of these parsnips. They were a dull red instead of a healthy purple, and when he broke one open, instead of being white it was a sickly gray.

"Babe!" shouted Little Meery. "Keep away from those parsnips!"

But Babe wouldn't be stopped; he hadn't tasted a parsnip for months, and the very look of that promising pile maddened him. Little Meery tried to block him, to stand between the hungry creature and death. Babe lowered his head. He liked Little Meery, and he didn't want to trample him. Instead, Babe filled his cavernous lungs, gave one long snort, and blew Little Meery out of the way.

Little Meery was desperate. But he wasn't defeated. He knew how much Babe meant to Paul; even if it killed him, he determined to save the Blue Ox. But how?

Suddenly Little Meery thought of the bees—the bees that had grown as big as eagles! He could hear their humming, like heavy engines, in the locked hives. There was anger in that humming, for the bees had been robbed of their honey, and the wildflowers of Wisconsin had been withered by the frost. Little Meery picked himself up and stealthily approached the hives. He lifted the latch a few inches—a foot—three feet—until the door stood wide open.

The humming changed to a furious buzz; the buzzing became a raging roar. And the bees, thundering out of the hive, lit out for Babe. They flew straight as only a bee can fly—but it was a beeline of eagles, bees with thundering, widespread wings and beaks that tore the flesh. Babe plunged left and right to avoid them. But they came at him like bullets. A hundred at a time they settled on him, zooming as they plunged. Babe shook his enormous hide, reared up on his hind legs, rolled over. But, though he crushed half a hundred giant bees, the others held fast. And another hundred flew to the attack. Babe swished his mighty tail, kicked up a cloud of solid dust, and plunged into a bed of briars. But the bees wouldn't be thrown off. They buzzed and roared; Babe blew and bellowed.

By this time the camp was boiling over. The loggers jumped into their boots; the farmers, who had unloaded the crop, picked up shovels and pitchforks. Phil Plenty, who had come along with the first wagonload, sprang at Little Meery.

"What right have you got to interfere?" shouted Phil. "Who told you to loose these bees?"

"That's my business!" Little Meery shouted back. "And your business is to feed Babe—not to poison him!"

"What!" screamed Phil, frightened and furious that his plan had been discovered. "I'll show you whose business is whose!" And he tackled Little Meery around the waist.

That was all the men needed.

"Hurrah for Little Meery!" yelled the loggers, squaring off at the farmers.

"Give it to him, Phil!" yelled the farmers, mixing it with the loggers.

Never had there been such an uproar. The crazy whoops, the battling men, the clash of poles and pitchforks, the violent buzzing of the monstrous bees, the wild bellowing of Babe—the noise was deafening. The loggers and farmers forgot they were human beings and fought like beasts; the beasts forgot they were animals and fought like men. There was blood on the ground when a fringe of pine trees was snapped apart and Paul appeared.

"What's going on here?" said Paul. He didn't have to raise his voice, for everything was suddenly quiet. The men stood their ground sheepishly; Babe lowered his head and pawed the earth; the bees flew softly back to their hive.

"How did it happen? Who started it?"

For a while no one answered. Then Little Meery spoke. "It's my fault. I guess I should have waited. Or spoken more civil-like to Phil Plenty. Or something. But when I realized that he had a grudge against Babe, and that he was trying to kill the Blue Ox with poisoned parsnips———"

"Kill Babe!" shouted Paul, losing control of himself. "With poisoned parsnips! You did right, Little Meery, exactly right. I'm grateful to you—and," here he slapped his thighs and laughed, "Babe should be grateful to those bees. As for that scoundrel, Phil Plenty, we'll make him eat those poisoned vegetables, every one down to the last parsnip! And he might as well begin now. Did you hear me, Phil Plenty?"

But there was no reply. As soon as Phil caught sight of Paul's boots crashing among the trees, he disappeared. Some say he jumped into the lake and swam back to Vermont. Some say he ran west and is still running. No one expected him back, and no one ever mentioned his name again.

Charles

Shirley Jackson

The day my son Laurie started kindergarten he renounced corduroy overalls with bibs and began wearing blue jeans with a belt; I watched him go off the first morning with the older girl next door, seeing clearly that an era of my life was ended, my sweet-voiced nursery-school tot replaced by a long-trousered, swaggering character who forgot to stop at the corner and wave good-bye to me.

He came home the same way, the front door slamming open, his cap on the floor, and the voice suddenly become raucous shouting, "Isn't anybody *here?*"

At lunch he spoke insolently to his father, spilled his baby sister's milk, and remarked that his teacher said we were not to take the name of the Lord in vain.

"How *was* school today?" I asked, elaborately casual.

"All right," he said.

"Did you learn anything?" his father asked.

Laurie regarded his father coldly. "I didn't learn nothing," he said.

"Anything," I said. "Didn't learn anything."

"The teacher spanked a boy, though," Laurie said, addressing his bread and butter. "For being fresh," he added, with his mouth full.

"What did he do?" I asked. "Who was it?"

Laurie thought. "It was Charles," he said. "He was fresh. The teacher spanked him and made him stand in a corner. He was awfully fresh."

"What did he do?" I asked again, but Laurie slid off his chair, took a cookie, and left, while his father was still saying, "See here, young man."

The next day Laurie remarked at lunch, as soon as he sat down, "Well, Charles was bad again today." He grinned enormously and said, "Today Charles hit the teacher."

"Good heavens," I said, mindful of the Lord's name, "I suppose he got spanked again?"

"He sure did," Laurie said. "Look up," he said to his father.

"What?" his father said, looking up.

"Look down," Laurie said. "Look at my thumb. Gee, you're dumb." He began to laugh insanely.

"Why did Charles hit the teacher?" I asked quickly.

"Because she tried to make him color with red crayons," Laurie said. "Charles wanted to color with green crayons so he hit the teacher and she spanked him and said nobody play with Charles but everybody did."

The third day—it was Wednesday of the first week—Charles bounced a see-saw on the head of a little girl and made her bleed, and the teacher made him stay inside all during recess. Thursday Charles had to stand in a corner during story-time because he kept pounding his feet on the floor. Friday Charles was deprived of blackboard privileges because he threw chalk.

On Saturday I remarked to my husband, "Do you

think kindergarten is too unsettling for Laurie? All his toughness, and bad grammar, and this Charles boy sounds like such a bad influence."

"It'll be all right," my husband said reassuringly. "Bound to be people like Charles in the world. Might as well meet them now as later."

On Monday Laurie came home late, full of news. "Charles," he shouted as he came up the hill; I was waiting anxiously on the front steps. "Charles," Laurie yelled all the way up the hill, "Charles was bad again."

"Come right in," I said, as soon as he came close enough. "Lunch is waiting."

"You know what Charles did?" he demanded, following me through the door. "Charles yelled so in school they sent a boy in from first grade to tell the teacher she had to make Charles keep quiet, and so Charles had to stay after school. And so all the children stayed to watch him.

"What did he do?" I asked.

"He just sat there," Laurie said, climbing into his chair at the table. "Hi, Pop, y'old dust mop."

"Charles had to stay after school today," I told my husband. "Everyone stayed with him."

"What does this Charles look like?" my husband asked Laurie. "What's his other name?"

"He's bigger than me," Laurie said. "And he doesn't have any rubbers and he doesn't ever wear a jacket."

Monday night was the first Parent-Teachers meeting, and only the fact that the baby had a cold kept me from going; I wanted passionately to meet Charles's mother. On Tuesday Laurie remarked suddenly, "Our teacher had a friend come to see her in school today."

"Charles's mother?" my husband and I asked simultaneously.

"Naaah," Laurie said scornfully. "It was a man who came and made us do exercises, we had to touch our toes. Look." He climbed down from his chair and squatted down and touched his toes. "Like this," he said. He got solemnly back into his chair and said, picking up his fork, "Charles didn't even *do* exercises."

"That's fine," I said heartily. "Didn't Charles want to do exercises?"

"Naaah," Laurie said. "Charles was so fresh to the teacher's friend he wasn't *let* do exercises."

"Fresh again?" I said.

"He kicked the teacher's friend," Laurie said. "The teacher's friend told Charles to touch his toes like I just did and Charles kicked him."

"What are they going to do about Charles, do you suppose?" Laurie's father asked him.

Laurie shrugged elaborately. "Throw him out of school, I guess," he said.

Wednesday and Thursday were routine; Charles yelled during story hour and hit a boy in the stomach and made him cry. On Friday Charles stayed after school again and so did all the other children.

With the third week of kindergarten Charles was an institution in our family; the baby was being a Charles when she cried all afternoon; Laurie did a Charles when he filled his wagon full of mud and pulled it through the kitchen; even my husband, when he caught his elbow in the telephone cord and pulled telephone, ashtray, and a bowl of flowers off the table, said, after the first minute, "Looks like Charles."

During the third and fourth weeks it looked like a reformation in Charles; Laurie reported grimly at lunch on Thursday of the third week, "Charles was so good today the teacher gave him an apple."

"What?" I said, and my husband added warily, "You mean Charles?"

"Charles," Laurie said. "He gave the crayons around and he picked up the books afterward and the teacher said he was her helper."

"What happened?" I asked incredulously.

"He was her helper, that's all," Laurie said, and shrugged.

"Can this be true, about Charles?" I asked my husband that night. "Can something like this happen?"

"Wait and see," my husband said cynically. "When you've got a Charles to deal with, this may mean he's only plotting."

He seemed to be wrong. For over a week Charles was the teacher's helper; each day he handed things out and he picked things up; no one had to stay after school.

"The P.T.A. meeting's next week again," I told my husband one evening. "I'm going to find Charles's mother there."

"Ask her what happened to Charles," my husband said. "I'd like to know."

"I'd like to know myself," I said.

On Friday of that week things were back to normal. "You know what Charles did today?" Laurie demanded at the lunch table, in a voice slightly awed. "He told a little girl to say a word and she said it and the teacher washed her mouth out with soap and Charles laughed."

"What word?" his father asked unwisely, and Laurie

said, "I'll have to whisper it to you, it's so bad." He got down off his chair and went around to his father. His father bent his head down and Laurie whispered joyfully. His father's eyes widened.

"Did Charles tell the little girl to say *that*?" he asked respectfully.

"She said it *twice*," Laurie said. "Charles told her to say it *twice*."

"What happened to Charles?" my husband asked.

"Nothing," Laurie said. "He was passing out the crayons."

Monday morning Charles abandoned the little girl and said the evil word himself three or four times, getting his mouth washed out with soap each time. He also threw chalk.

My husband came to the door with me that evening as I set out for the P.T.A. meeting. "Invite her over for a cup of tea after the meeting," he said. "I want to get a look at her."

"If only she's there," I said prayerfully.

"She'll be there," my husband said. "I don't see how they could hold a P.T.A. meeting without Charles's mother."

At the meeting I sat restlessly, scanning each comfortable matronly face, trying to determine which one hid the secret of Charles. None of them looked to me haggard enough. No one stood up in the meeting and apologized for the way her son had been acting. No one mentioned Charles.

After the meeting I identified and sought out Laurie's kindergarten teacher. She had a plate with a cup of tea and a piece of chocolate cake; I had a plate with a cup of tea and a piece of marshmallow cake. We maneuvered up to one another cautiously, and smiled.

"I've been so anxious to meet you," I said. "I'm Laurie's mother."

"We're all so interested in Laurie," she said.

"Well, he certainly likes kindergarten," I said. "He talks about it all the time."

"We had a little trouble adjusting, the first week or so," she said primly, "but now he's a fine little helper. With occasional lapses, of course."

"Laurie usually adjusts very quickly," I said. "I suppose this time it's Charles's influence."

"Charles?"

"Yes," I said, laughing, "you must have your hands full in that kindergarten, with Charles."

"Charles?" she said. "We don't have any Charles in the kindergarten."

Little Moron Jokes

Did you hear about the little moron who
stayed up all night to study for a blood test.
had all his teeth pulled out so he could have more gum
    to chew.
took the bus home, but his mother made him take it
    back.
took a ruler to bed so he could see how long he slept.
ate five pennies so he could see the change in himself.
ran around the bed trying to catch some sleep.
got off the bus backwards because he heard a lady was
    going to grab his seat when he got off.
went into the closet to change his mind.
went into the living room because he thought he was
    going to die.
thought Manuel Labor was the president of Mexico.
took a hammer to bed so he could hit the hay.
moved to the city because he heard the country was at
    war.
thought shoes grow on shoe trees.
wouldn't buy a dictionary until it was made into a
    movie.
took the rug off the floor so he could see the floor
    show.

threw his clock out the window so he could see time
  fly.
thought a hot dog was a stolen poodle.
slept in the fireplace so he could sleep like a log.
cut a hole in the top of his umbrella to see if it was
  raining out.
got his name when the bus driver said, "No more on."

Why did the little moron lie in the sun for hours?
He wanted to be the toast of the town.

Why did the little moron rob a glue factory?
He wanted to be a stick-up man.

Why did the little moron buy clothes for his lawyer?
He heard the lawyer had lost his suit.

Why did the little moron put iodine on the window?
He heard it had a pane.

Why did the little moron stand on the ladder to sing?
He wanted to reach the high notes.

Why did the little moron flood the football field?
He wanted to be a sub.

Why did the little moron become a bus driver?
He wanted to tell people where to get off.

Why did the little moron put a clock under his bed?
He wanted to sleep over time.

Why did the little moron buy a short coat?
He heard it would be long before he got another one.

Why did the little moron climb up on the roof?
He heard the drinks were on the house.

Why did the little moron chew gum on the train?
Because the engine said, "Chew, chew."

Why aren't there any more little moron stories?
Because he was in a submarine and decided to open the
   window.

7.

1950-1959

America Laughs at Itself

Cartoon—Paul Peter Porges
She Shall Have Music—Max Shulman
Gracie Talks About her Relatives—Burns and Allen
No Time for Sergeants—Mac Hyman
Chief White Halfoat—Joseph Heller
Dental or Mental, I say It's Spinach—S. J. Perel-
   man
Comic Definitions

Introduction

Despite the war in Korea and the witch hunts of Senator McCarthy, Americans in the fifties were experiencing an economic boom and moving to the suburbs in droves to build a private peace in a public world increasingly beyond their control.

The revolutionary development of the decade was television. It was developed during the late 1940s, and by 1959 most people were able to watch the programs on their own sets. Humor began to depend upon personality, upon the twitch of an eyebrown that broke viewers up before the comedian even opened his mouth. With a television set in nearly every home, comedy shows began to exploit everyday situations familiar to everyone, and the viewers were participators as well. This kind of humor had a bland and homogenized quality.

But there were also comedians who directed their sardonic jokes to the loser, the alienated, in our society. Their stories concerned antiheroes, and they made a joke of the fact that there was no happy ending.

The fine art of debunking became a weapon of humorists against big business, politicians, advertising, and the incomprehensible advances made by science.

"Well . . . back to the old drawing board!"

Paul Peter Porges, 1

She Shall Have Music

Max Shulman

Ski-U-Mah was in a bad way.

"Something's got to be done," said Dewey Davenport, the editor. "There's no time to waste. School starts in two weeks."

"Let's hear from the circulation manager," said Boyd Phelps, the associate editor.

They looked at me.

"Oh, Pansy, Pansy!" I cried.

Dewey put a sympathetic arm around my shoulder. "Get hold of yourself Dobie," he said kindly. "Pansy is gone."

"Gone," I sighed. "Gone."

"And Ski-U-Mah," he continued, "is in trouble."

"You must forget Pansy," said Boyd. "Try to think about Ski-U-Mah."

"I'll try," I whispered bravely.

"That's my boy," said Dewey, giving me a manly squeeze. "Now, Dobie, you're the circulation manager. Have you got any ideas to build circulation?"

But I wasn't listening. Pansy's face was before me. The fragrance of her hair was in my nostrils, and I thought my heart would be rent asunder. Pansy, Pansy, lost and taken from me! "Pansy," I moaned.

"Dobie, she's not dead," said Dewey with a touch of annoyance. "Don't be so emotional."

"I'm an emotional type," I cried, and indeed I was. That had been the seat of my trouble with Pansy—my inability to contain my emotions in her presence. The very sight of her had made me spastic with delight. I had twitched, quivered, shaken, jumped, and whirled my arms in concentric circles. Pansy had looked kindly upon my seizures, but her father, a large, hostile man named Mr. Hammer, had taken an opposite view. He had regarded me with a mixture of loathing and panic, and finally, fearing for his daughter's safety, he had sent her away from me.

I had met Pansy the year before at the University of Minnesota where we had both been freshmen. I had been immediately smitten. And who would not have been? What healthy male would not have succumbed to her wise but frolicsome eyes, her firm but succulent lips, her sturdy but graceful throat, her youthful but mature form? What man could have resisted her manifold graces, her myriad charms? Certainly not I.

I plunged headlong into the pursuit of Pansy, and I am pleased to report that my suit met with success. After she overcame her initial alarm at my exuberance, her affection for me burgeoned until it matched mine for her. Then I made a mistake: I asked to meet her folks.

"Gee, I don't know, Dobie," she said doubtfully. "Maybe we'd better wait awhile. I'm not sure how you and Daddy will get along."

"If he's your father, I'll love him," I replied, nibbling her fingers ecstatically.

"Maybe so," she said, "But I'm worried about what

he'll think of you. He's a gruff, sober type, and—no offense, Dobie—you're kind of nuts."

"Nonsense," I cried, leaping goatlike around her. "Take me to him."

"All right," she said with a conspicuous lack of enthusiam. "But, Dobie, listen. Try to make your outbursts as minor as possible, will you? Nothing massive if you can help it."

"Don't worry about a thing," I assured her, and we went forthwith to her costly home in South Minneapolis.

I must say that I have never behaved quite so calmly as on my first meeting with Mr. and Mrs. Hammer. I did not leap or spin; I did not cavort, dance, kick, whistle, or roll. Perhaps I twitched a few times, and I blinked a bit, and once I wrapped my hands around my head, but otherwise I was the very model of sedateness.

I cannot say, however that the Hammers were impressed with my composure. Mrs. Hammer showed only slight evidences of nervousness—just an occasional shudder—but Mr. Hammer was openly agitated. He kept casting me looks of wild surmise; several times he inquired pointedly about my health. When I finally made my goodbyes, he was flagrantly relieved.

"Well, what did they think of me?" I asked Pansy when I saw her on campus the next day.

"Mother seemed disinclined to discuss you," Pansy replied, "but Daddy was quite frank. He said you ought to be locked up."

"Hm," I said glumly, but my spirits instantly revived. "Don't worry, Pansy," I said confidently. "I will win him."

Overriding Pansy's earnest protests, I continued to call on her at home. The results were not what I had hoped. Her mother contrived to be absent whenever I came. Her father's attitude toward me progressed from dismay to consternation; his color evolved from a brackish white to a mottled purple. It seemed that there was nothing I could do to please him. My friendly grimaces only served to infuriate him. Whenever I gave him a jovial slap on the back, he recoiled in horror. It got so that the mere sight of me would set him whimpering. "No good will come of all this," I told myself darkly.

I was right. Mr. Hammer sent Pansy away from me. Instead of letting her return to the University of Minnesota for her second year, he shipped her off to New York City. There she was to live with her Aunt Naomi, a flinty old spinster, and attend Barnard College. Aunt Naomi had been instructed by Mr. Hammer to reject all phone calls and destroy all letters coming from me.

And now here I was in the Ski-U-Mah office, separated from my true love by half a continent. If only I had some money, I would have flown to her, but I was poor as a church-mouse and twice as miserable.

"Dobie," said Dewey Davenport sharply. "Will you pay attention? Ski-U-Mah may have to close this year. We've only got two weeks before school starts. We need circulation. That's your job, remember?"

"Pansy," I said, biting my lip. "Pansy."

"Ah, what's the use?" said Boyd Phelps dejectedly. "Even if Dobie had any ideas, it wouldn't help. Let's face it, Dewey. Ski-U-Mah is a dead duck. The day of the college humor magazine is over—not only at Minnesota, but everywhere. College kids have outgrown all that rah-rah stuff. The war, the A-bomb, the

H-bomb—who's thinking about fun and jokes these days?"

"Nuts," replied Dewey. "College kids are still college kids. They're still smooching and driving convertibles and cutting classes and looking for laughs."

"Not like they used to," said Boyd.

"Yes," Dewey insisted. "Here, I'll give you an example. Remember last year when Benny Goodman played a dance at the gym? They had the biggest turnout in the history of the university. Does that sound like everyone is sitting around moping?"

Yes, I thought, a soft smile playing on my lips, yes, I remembered that dance. Pansy and I had gone together. Oh, how we danced, how we stomped, how we whirled, how we hopped, how we—CLANG! A bell sounded in my head with the noise of a thousand alarms. An idea had come to me, an overpoweringly perfect idea! Everything was solved. *Everything!*

"I've got it!" I cried, jumping up and down. "I've got it!"

Dewey and Boyd looked at me askance.

"That's our answer," I said eagerly. "That's how we'll get subscriptions for Ski-U-Mah. We'll hold a dance."

"I don't get it," confessed Dewey.

"Look," I said. "We'll hire a big-name band— Benny Goodman or Tommy Dorsey or somebody like that. Then instead of charging a dollar for a ticket to the dance as they usually do, we'll charge two dollars. The extra dollar will be for a year's subscription to Ski-U-Mah. It's a package deal, don't you see?"

Dewey and Boyd considered the idea. "Not bad, not bad," said Boyd.

"No, it isn't," Dewey agreed. "It's a fine idea.

There's only one hitch. Have we got enough money in our treasury to hire a big-name band?"

"We've got exactly one thousand dollars," said Boyd.

Dewey shook his head. "Not enough."

"We could try," said Boyd. "Why don't we write a letter to the booking office in New York and see what they say?"

"No, no," I cried quickly. That wasn't what I had in mind at all. A trip to New York was the most important part of my plan—to see Pansy again, to live again, to be a whole man again. But, of course, I did not intend to mention *that* to Dewey and Boyd.

"Don't send a letter," I said. "They'll only turn you down. You can't expect them to send Goodman or Dorsey all the way to Minneapolis for a thousand dollars—unless, of course, some young clean-cut fellow appeared in person and persuaded them."

"You, for instance?" said Dewey.

"Not to brag," I said, lowering my eyes modestly, "but you will go far to find another as young and clean-cut as I."

"And you think they'd listen to you at the booking agency?" asked Dewey.

"I'm sure of it," I declared. "I'll come up there all neat and tweedy with my cowlick standing up and a lump in my throat and I'll tell them all about our great Ski-U-Mah tradition and how the magazine is in trouble and how everything depends on them, and then I'll look up at them, trusting-like, with my eyes shining and a crooked little smile on my face. How can they resist me?"

I took a stance and showed Dewey and Boyd what I meant.

"He *does* look kind of appealing," Boyd admitted.

"Yes, he does," said Dewey, examining me minutely.

I nodded energetically.

Dewey waved a forefinger under my nose. "Now listen, Dobie, your expenses have to come out of this thousand dollars, so don't waste a cent. You'll travel by bus and you'll sleep at the Y.M.C.A. Eat as little as possible. Do your business as soon as you get to New York and then come right back. Understand?"

"Yes, yes, yes," I said, clapping my hands rapidly. I was going to Pansy, to Pansy, to Pansy! Oh, happy day! Oh, kind fate!

The next morning Dewey and Boyd took me down to the Minneapolis bus depot and put me on a bus for New York. I got off the bus in St. Paul and transferred to an airplane. A tedious bus journey was not to be borne; I had to get to Pansy quickly. I felt a little guilty about spending the extra fare, but after all, twenty or thirty dollars would hardly make any difference when I came to hire a band.

As soon as I landed at LaGuardia Field, I rushed to the telephones. I looked up Aunt Naomi's number and dialed it with trembling fingers. An unfriendly feminine voice answered. "Hello?"

"Hello," I said. "Is Miss Pansy Hammer there?"

"Who is calling?" asked the voice suspiciously.

"This is Mr. Johnson. I am the dean of Barnard College."

"You sound awfully young to be a dean," said doubting old Aunt Naomi.

"Yes, don't I?" I replied with a hollow laugh. "In many quarters I am known as 'The Boy Dean.' . . . But enough of this chitchat. I'm a very busy dean. Please put Miss Hammer on."

There was a short pause and I heard Pansy's voice.

"Pansy!" I cried, vibrating joyously in the phone booth. "Pansy, it's Dobie Gillis. I've come to you, my darling. I'm here in New York."

I heard a sharp intake of breath and then she said in a carefully controlled tone, "Why yes, Dean. When do you want to see me?"

"Smart girl," I said approvingly. "Can you meet me in an hour at the airlines terminal building in New York?"

"I'll be there," she said. "Goodbye, Dean."

Rubbing my hands gleefully, I got into the airlines limousine and rode to New York. I was at the terminal building in thirty minutes. That left another thirty minutes to wait before Pansy would arrive. I was much too agitated to sit still so I decided to go out for a short walk. I skipped down Forty-second Street and turned up Fifth Avenue. The gaily decorated shopwindows matched my festive mood, and soon I was singing lustily. As I passed a florist's shop, my attention was seized by a display of orchids in the window. No ordinary orchids these, but blooms as white and soft and lovely as Pansy herself. I went into the store.

A clerk slithered toward me. "M'sieu?" he lisped.

"I would like a dozen of those orchids," I cried, "for the loveliest girl in the world."

"*Quel sentiment!*" he exclaimed, embracing me.

"Quickly," I said, disengaging myself. "She comes."

He swished into action and in a trice he had fashioned a corsage that made me limp with rapture. "That will be one hundred dollars," he said.

I turned ashen.

"A glass of water?" asked the clerk. "A light wine, perhaps?"

I shook my head, for already I was recovering. After all, what difference would a hundred dollars make when it came to hiring the band? The whole deal was to be based on my personal appeal anyhow. In fact, the less money I had, the more pathetic I would be. And besides, it would be worth a hundred dollars to see Pansy's face when I gave her the corsage—even if the hundred dollars was not mine. Smiling, I handed the clerk the money and raced back to the terminal building.

She was waiting for me. Fifty feet separated us when I first spied her. I covered the distance in three great bounds. "My darling, my angel, my dove!" I cried, kissing her with random accuracy.

"Dobie," she said simply.

We clung.

"A corsage," I said, handing her the orchids.

"Oh, they're lovely. . . . But it's kind of big for a corsage, isn't it, Dobie?"

"I'll fix that," I said and draped the orchids around her neck like a Derby winner.

We laughed. Then, suddenly serious, I clutched her again. "I've missed you so much, Pansy."

She nuzzled my jowl. "And I you," she confessed.

"Is there no chance that your father will let you come back to Minnesota?"

She shook her head. "No. I start classes at Barnard next week."

"Shall I survive this year?" I croaked hoarsely, smiting my forehead.

"I know," she said softly. "It's going to be awful."
She wept, nor were my eyes dry.

"But away with this gloom!" I cried. "At least we
will have a little time together. Let us be gay. Let us
taste all the joys that this great city has to offer."

"Heigh-ho," she replied airily and linked her pretty
round arm in mine.

Some may censure me for my activities on that evening, and I cannot really defend myself. Admittedly
the expenditure of two hundred dollars of Ski-U-Mah
funds was not an honorable act. I can only say this: I
did not know when I would see Pansy again; there was
money in my pocket; the town was full of pleasures;
and even under the best of circumstances, I cannot
think clearly in Pansy's presence. Call me wayward if
you will; that was the way things were.

We had cocktails at the Plaza. We had dinner at 21.
We saw *South Pacific*. We had supper at the Stork. We
danced at El Morocco. We drove four times around
Central Park in a hansom. After I took Pansy home, I
checked into the Waldorf. No lesser hostelry would
suit my exalted mood.

In the morning, of course, things were different. I
lay between the Waldorf's excellent sheets jack-knifed
with panic. It took a long time before I was able to get
up and count my money. Then, having discovered that
my funds totaled slightly over six hundred dollars, I
oozed to the floor in a moaning mound. An hour was
spent in this position. At length I rallied myself. There
was nothing to do but go down to the booking agency
and try to get a band for six hundred dollars.

I prepared myself carefully. I yanked my cowlick
until it stood like a mast on my scalp. I buffed my face

until it shone like a Baldwin apple. I practiced digging my toe into the rug. I stood before the mirror and ran through my repertory of winsome expressions. Then I went down to the booking agency.

The booking agency occupied one large, shabby office. Part of the office was a waiting room; the other part, separated by a waist-high railing, was the business office. Seated on a bench in the waiting room were six huge, villainous-looking women. At the desk behind the railing sat a cadaverous, blue-jowled man with eyes like two bits of anthracite. The six women were staring dully at the floor as I entered. They looked at me with momentary interest, then sighed and returned their gaze to the floor. I approached the man behind the railing.

"How do you do?" I said with a fetching smile. "I'm Dobie Gillis from the University of Minnesota Ski-U-Mah."

He gave me a quick appraisal with his anthracite eyes and said nothing.

"I'd like to book a band for a dance at the university on September 14. I had in mind someone like Benny Goodman or Tommy Dorsey."

"How much loot you got?" asked the man.

"I beg your pardon?"

"Money. How much?"

"First," I said, smiling warmly, "I'd like to tell you a little about Ski-U-Mah. It's one of the finest traditions at the University of Minnesota. Yes, indeed. We all have a soft spot in our hearts for Ski-U-Mah out there. We certainly do."

"How much loot?"

"Ski-U-Mah, you'll be distressed to hear, has fallen

on evil days. But now, with your co-operation, we believe we can save it. I know, of course, that sentiment and business are not supposed to mix, but I always say, scratch a businessman and you'll find a heart of pure gold."

"Kid, come on already. How much loot?"

"Six hundred dollars," I said, turning a look upon him that would melt a stone.

"Goodbye, kid," he said.

"Vaughan Monroe would do," I said, tugging my cowlick.

"Kid," he said, "you got rocks in your head?"

"Perhaps," I said in a cracking treble, "you could suggest somebody?"

"Nobody," he said flatly, "will go to Minneapolis for six hundred dollars."

"Ahem, ahem." The sound came from behind me. I turned and saw the largest of the six women on the bench rise and approach me with a gigantic grin.

"Kid," said the man at the desk, "you're in luck. This is Happy Stella Kowalski and her Schottische Five. They just happen to be between bookings right now."

"Pleased to make your acquaintance, hey," said Happy Stella crushing my hand in hers. The Schottische Five stood up and grinned fatly.

"You are a band?" I asked nervously.

"The best," roared Happy Stella. "Ask Al."

"The best," confirmed the man at the desk. "They play more Lithuanian weddings than any band on the entire Atlantic Seaboard."

"We're a riot, hey," confessed Stella, prodding me with her outsized forefinger. "We wear funny hats.

We black our teeth. We play washboards, gaspipes, pots and pans, all kinds of funny stuff. We fracture the people."

"You mustn't take this unkindly, Happy Stella," I said, "But I've never heard of you."

"Kid, where you been?" asked Al. "This is the hottest combination in New York. You don't know how lucky you are to catch 'em between bookings."

I scratched my head uncertainly. "And they'll come for six hundred dollars?"

"Ordinarily, no," said Al. "For Ski-U-Mah, yes."

He whipped out a contract, gave me a pen, and guided my hand over the dotted line. Then I shook hands with Al and Happy Stella and the Schottische Five—Rutka, Sletka, Dombra, Simka, and Majeska—and left the office with a breast full of misgivings.

I had not done well; there was no gainsaying it. For a moment I toyed with the idea of not going back to Minneapolis, but finally dismissed the thought as cowardly. Besides, I didn't have enough money left to stay in New York. I went to the bus station, bought a ticket home with my remaining resources, and invested my last dime in a good-by phone call to Pansy.

Aunt Naomi answered. "Hello," I said, "this is Mr. Johnson, the Boy Dean. I want to talk to Miss Hammer."

"I have called Barnard College," said Aunt Naomi icily. "There is no Mr. Johnson on the faculty. You are Dobie Gillis, and if you try to communicate with Pansy again I will call the police."

"Please, Aunt Naomi," I could hear Pansy saying, "just let me say goodby to him."

"Very well," said Aunt Naomi. "But this is the last time, you understand?"

Pansy came on the phone. "How are you, Dobie dear?"

Fine," I lied. There was no use to afflict her with my misery.

"Did you get Benny Goodman for your dance?"

"No," I said with a wan smile, "I got somebody better. Happy Stella Kowalski and her Schottische Five."

"Who?"

"It's a sensational new all-girl band. They fracture the people."

"That's nice, dear. When are you leaving?"

"In a few minutes."

"Oh, how I wish I were going back with you! I'll miss you so much, Dobie, so very much."

"Me too."

She sobbed briefly.

"Don't cry, dear," I soothed. "Maybe we'll be together soon."

"It can't be soon enough. When do you think you'll get back to New York?"

"Not," I said, "in the foreseeable future."

"Oh, Dobie!" she wailed.

"Goodbye, Pansy, dear heart. I love you."

Gently I hung up the telephone and walked into the bus for Minneapolis.

Dewey and Boyd were waiting for me at the Minneapolis station. At first I tried to bluff it out. "Great news, fellows!" I shouted. "I booked Happy Stella Kowalski and her Schottische Five. What a coup for Ski-U-Mah!"

"Who?" said Dewey and Boyd with double horror.

I could not go on with it. Suddenly the truth came pouring from my lips, the whole horrible story. "But I'll pay back the money I spent," I said in conclusion. "I'll pay it back somehow."

"I know you will, Dobie," said Dewey wearily, without anger. "That's not the point. What happens to Ski-U-Mah now? How do we get anybody to buy tickets for Happy Stella Kowalski?"

"They'll close the magazine this year if we don't make a profit," said Boyd.

I know," I replied miserably. "I'm just a no-good rat."

Dewey put his arm around my slumping shoulders. "All right Dobie. What's done is done. Now the only thing left is to try to sell some dance tickets."

And try we did. We collared everybody on campus; we applied all possible pressures. Our efforts were greeted with curt refusals, sometimes with astonishment. "Happy Stella who?" people would ask. When the night of the dance came around, we had sold exactly 150 tickets to an enrollment of 20,000 students.

At 7:30 on the night of the dance I was in the gymnasium disconsolately hanging bunting. Dewey was sitting on the bandstand with his chin in his hand. Boyd had gone down to the railroad station to pick up Happy Stella Kowalski and her Schottische Five, who were due to arrive at eight o'clock. Suddenly a large, purple-faced man came running wildly into the gymnasium—Mr. Hammer, Pansy's father.

He spied me on top of the ladder. "You!" he roared and shook me down like a ripe plum. "What have you done with her?"

"Hello, Mr. Hammer. Nice to see you. Done with whom?"

"You know very well who. Where's Pansy? Her aunt told me you saw her in New York. Now where is she?"

"Isn't she in New York?"

"Gillis, I'll strangle you," he yelled, lunging at me.

Dewey thrust himself hastily between us. "What's wrong, Mr. Hammer?" he asked.

"Pansy disappeared from her aunt's apartment in New York two days ago. Gillis engineered the whole thing. He's got her hidden someplace. I'm calling the police. I'm charging him with abduction." All this delivered in a deafening bellow.

Dewey turned to me. "Dobie, tell the truth. Do you know anything about this?"

"So help me, Dewey," I cried earnestly, "not a thing."

You're lying, you kidnapper," screamed Mr. Hammer. "I'm calling the police. Where is she?"

"Mr. Hammer, be reasonable," said Dewey. "Dobie's been here for more than a week. How could he have kidnapped Pansy?"

"He's got accomplices. He's a fiend. I knew he should have been locked up the minute I laid eyes on him. I'm calling the police."

At this point Boyd came walking in with Stella Kowalski and her Schottische Five. They were dressed in motley dirndls about the size of pyramidal tents. On their heads they wore hideous hats with ratty plumes. Under their arms they carried washboards, pipes, pots, plungers, and assorted hardware. Their front teeth were blacked out.

We stood and stared at them, even Mr. Hammer. Then suddenly I saw that the Schottische Five were six, and the sixth one was not a huge, gross cow moose of a woman. She was slender and fair and beautiful even with blacked-out teeth. She was Pansy!

"Pansy!" The cry escaped my lips.

"Aha!" roared Mr. Hammer. "Caught you red-handed." There was a telephone on the wall nearby. He seized it. "Police!" he shouted into the mouthpiece. "Send the patrol wagon. Send the riot squad. Send everything you've got!"

Happy Stella strode over and grabbed Mr. Hammer by the lapels. "What's with you?" she said dangerously.

"You'll find out when you're behind bars," replied Mr. Hammer, trying vainly to loose himself.

"Oh, you must be the old man," said Happy Stella. "Shame on you." She shook him until his eyes rolled freely in their sockets.

"Assault and battery," mumbled Mr. Hammer. "Kidnapping plus assault and battery. That's what I'm charging you with."

Pansy stepped forward. "There was no kidnapping," she said firmly. "I went to Happy Stella and asked her to take me with her. I thought Aunt Naomi might catch me if I tried running away alone."

"Don't say anything, Pansy," warned Mr. Hammer. "They've probably got you drugged."

"I am not drugged," said Pansy, stamping her foot. "I have never thought so clearly in my life."

She walked over and took my arm. "Daddy," she said with as much dignity as a girl can muster who has blackened-out teeth, "I love Dobie and I'm going to stay with him. If you send me to New York again, I'll run away again. I don't care where you send me, I'm not going to be kept apart from Dobie."

"Whatsa matter with you, hey?" demanded Happy Stella, giving Mr. Hammer another shake. "Can't you see these kids wanna be together? So what if Dobie is a little screwy? Who ain't?"

Mr. Hammer opened and closed his mouth several times, carp-fashion. "All right," he snarled at last. "All right. But, Pansy, you keep that maniac out of my house, do you hear? And if, God forbid, you should ever marry him, I don't want to hear about it."

Suddenly the street outside the gym was filled with the scream of sirens. The police Mr. Hammer had called were arriving. Car after car pulled up in front of the gym with a horrific screeching of tires. Dozens of cops with drawn guns came pouring into the gym. And behind the police came a mob of students, pressing in to see what the excitement was.

Dewey leaped up as though he had been stung. "Dobie, Boyd!" he yelled with wild excitement. "Get to the door. Don't let any students in unless they buy tickets. Here's how we save Ski-U-Mah."

We rushed forward and threw ourselves across the door. "Two dollars!" shouted Dewey to the mob. "Two dollars to come inside. Hurry, hurry, hurry!"

The students in the front ranks started to dig in their pockets for money, but the mob behind them surged forward. It looked for a moment as though Dewey, Boyd, and I would be swept aside. But Happy Stella came running to our aid with her Schottische Five. Buttressed by the musical Amazons, we were able to hold fast until the crowd got their money out.

Then we stood aside and let them rush through, throwing currency at us as they passed. The money showered over us, piled up on the floor around us.

It is difficult to describe what was happening inside the gym. I was not on the sinking *Titanic* or at the Battle of Gettysburg, but these, I think, are fair comparisons. All I can remember is humanity flooding in, filling the gym to the walls, and cops yelling and brandishing guns, and Mr. Hammer trying vainly to make explanations over the din, and Dewey cackling hysterically as he counted money.

It took about an hour before the cops left, casting foul looks at Mr. Hammer as they went. Then Dewey got up and made an announcement to the assemblage, telling them that they were at a dance. There was a little sullen muttering, but most of them took the news calmly. Then Happy Stella and her Schottische Five started to mount the bandstand.

"Miss Hammer," I said with a courtly bow to my true love, "May I have the honor of the first dance?"

"The second dance," she said. "I'm playing a washboard solo for the first dance."

She gave me a loving, black-toothed smile and joined the musicians.

Gracie Talks about her Relatives

Burns and Allen Television Show

GEORGE: What would you like to talk about to-night?

GRACIE: We could talk about my family.

GEORGE: All right.

GRACIE: My sister put in a new swimming pool last night, and we had more fun diving.

GEORGE: Yeah, that's great sport.

GRACIE: We'll have even more fun tomorrow when they put the water in.

GRACIE: My sister had a baby.

GEORGE: Boy or girl?

GRACIE: I don't know, and I can't wait to find out if I'm an aunt or an uncle.

GRACIE: My brother got one of those suits with two pairs of pants.

GEORGE: How does he like it?

GRACIE: Not so well. It's too hot wearing two pairs of pants.

GRACIE: My brother has a suit like yours. It's just the same.

GEORGE: Is that so?

GRACIE: Yes, only it hasn't any stripes. His is brown. It's more like a blue black, sort of yellow.

GEORGE: More like white!

GRACIE: That's it. A white suit, only yours is double-breasted and his is single-breasted and his has no pockets, and a bow on the side.

GEORGE: A bow on the side?

GRACIE: My sister wore it to a dance last night.

GEORGE: Your sister wore your brother's suit to a dance?

GRACIE: I haven't got a brother.

GEORGE: You haven't got a brother but your sister has?

GRACIE: It's a long story—pull up a chair. You see, when my sister and I were children, we were left orphans, and he was one of them.

GEORGE: This family of yours—did they live together?

GRACIE: Yes, my father, my uncle, my cousin, my brother, and my nephew used to sleep in one bed and my—

GEORGE: I'm surprised your grandfather didn't sleep with them.

GRACIE: He did. But he died, and they made him get up.

GEORGE: Say good-night Gracie.

GRACIE: Good-night Gracie.

refile

5L

cards

UNITED STATES --SOCIAL CONDITIONS --To 1855

309.1
Hof   Hofstadter, Richard.
             America at 1750; a social portrait/
         Random HOuse (c1971)
             293 p.

             1. United States --Social conditions --
         To 1855. I. Title.

No Time for Sergeants

Mac Hyman

The next day for inspection I cleaned up everything real white, except the tops which warnt supposed to be white, and Sergeant King went pacing all round the place examining bunks and getting wrinkles out of them and things like that, and telling everybody how to act, and just what the officers would do and everything. He worried a good bit about inspection like that, and he explained it to everybody again, and it happened just like he said it would too. The door opened and some Lieutenants and the Captain and the Colonel come in, and Sergeant King called out "Attention!" and everybody stood real stiff like they warnt breathing, and the Lieutenants peeped and sniffed around here and there, and the Captain went around looking over the men in their fresh uniforms, but the Colonel, *he* didnt waste no time at all—he only glanced at things and headed right past, coming for the latrine where I was standing at attention by myself, just like Sergeant King said he would do.

And he really was the most interested in latrines of any man you ever seen in your life. He was a nice old fellow too, gray-headed with a little moustache and looked like an uncle of mine, but I knowed it warnt as my uncle hadnt been drafted that I had heered—

anyhow, he headed right back for the latrine and went in and looked around, nodding his head and smiling, and seemed mighty pleased with it. And I was myself when I seen the look on his face and seen Sergeant King kind of cutting his eyes around at him. But I didnt want to take all the credit for myself, so when he came back by me on the way out, I said, "Colonel, I hope you like how we fixed up the latrine for you."

And when he turned to me and said, "What?" I said, "The reason it is so clean was mainly because of Sergeant King there. He's the one behind it all; I just done the cleaning. He said he had never seen a man in his life care more about latrines than you do, and that's the reason . . ."

"Attention!" the Captain yelled out. "You're at attention there!" and he came bounding over with his face all red like he was going to jump all over me.

But I didnt pay much attention to him because I warnt talking to him nohow, and besides the Colonel held up his hand at the Captain to shut him up, and then he looked at me for a while and asked me to go over what I had said again. So I did, and this time I really laid it on good too. I told him how Sergeant King had told me to clean it up so good because he had never seen a man in his life that would come back and stick his head right down in the bowls the way *he* done, and I think the Colonel kind of appreciated it too, because he looked around and said, "And which one is Sergeant King?"

So I pointed him out, though Sergeant King was right embarrassed and kind of white in the face, and the Colonel went over to speak with him for a minute. I couldnt make out what he said, though, because the

Captain begun talking to me, and seemed like he had got kind of interested in the latrine himself. He asked me if I had been doing all the cleaning by myself, and I told him, "Yessir, I been cleaning it for about two weeks now. I'm the permanent latrine orderly."

"You mean you havent even started *classification* yet? You've been here two weeks and havent even *started* . . . Oh, Sergeant King, step over here a minute, will you, when the Colonel finished speaking with you."

So we all kind of gathered around, the Colonel and the Captain and the Lieutenants and Sergeant King and myself, and had a real nice chat about it. They wanted to know about what I had been doing and I told them about the latrine and how Sergeant King let me work there, and how at first I was on KP for a while, and how nice Sergeant King had been to me, not making me bother with classification but letting me help wash his car and all; and we kept talking about it, only Sergeant King didnt say much but kept his head ducked down and kept blushing and acting modest and everything—anyhow, we talked and talked—and finally they got ready to leave, and the Captain said, "King, you come over and wait in the office. I want to talk to you a little while," and Sergeant King came to attention and said, "Yessir," so it all seemed to come off all right. And they was about the nicest bunch of officers I had ever seen and must have knowed me from somewhere too because just as they were leaving, the Captain looked at me and said, "You must be Stockdale."

And I said, "Yessir, that's right, but I dont recall meeting you . . ." but he didnt stay around no longer;

he only turned to the Lieutenant and said. "That one's Stockdale," and the Lieutenant looked at me and said, "Oh, yeah," and I said, "Yessir, that's right, but I don't recall meeting . . ." but they were already headed out about that time.

Anyhow, you could never tell how Sergeant King would feel about things, as changeable as he was, and when he come back from talking with the Captain, he was most *wild*-looking in a way. He stood in his room and kept blinking his eyes and shaking his head like he didnt even know I was there. "You didnt have to do it," he finally said. "You really didnt have to do that."

"I know it," I said. "But I didnt see no sense in me taking all the credit when it was your idea and all. You done a lot for me and I thought I could help out some and . . ."

But he kept shaking his head, and said, "Yes, but did you think that would be *helping* . . ." and then he stopped and rubbed his hands over his face and said, "Yes, I guess you would. I'm not surprised at all. But look here now, you dont have to help me out no more, see? I get along all right here. I got three stripes and my own barracks and I dont really need no help. You've done enough for me already. Look, you help somebody else out for a while. Look, I know a loud-mouthed, low-down, four-striper over in the orderly room, why dont you help *him* out a little bit? Why . . .?" But then he waved his hand like he didnt want to talk about it no more, and I said I would if I got the chance, but he waved his hand again and turned back around and said, "Look, Will, just forget everything else now. The main thing now is to get you *classified*. That's something we've *got* to do."

And then he seemed to get all upset about that too. He got to pacing up and down talking about it, seeming right anxious about it, and looking all worried again. So I tried to calm him down a bit; I said it probably didnt amount to much and that there really warnt that much to worry about because I liked the latrine fine and had just as soon stay right there as long as I was on the field.

But that seemed to upset him too. He said, "No, Will, no! You wouldnt want to spend the rest of your hitch here, would you? You want to get out and do something. Nosir, what we want to do is get you classified and shipped out of here, because the Captain said that if you didn't, you would stay right here and . . . Look, Will, if it's the last thing we ever do, I think we ought to get you classified. It's the *only* thing."

"Well, I was only thinking about the latrine and helping you out and . . ."

But he was the most upset I ever seen him. He said, "Nosir! Nosir! Absolutely not! The Captain said . . ." and then he got all jumbled up with it all. He shouted "Nosir!" a few more times, and then, "They'll ship you a thousand miles away from here!" and a lot of other stuff like that, getting more and more upset. And finally he wore himself out and just laid down on the bunk and covered up his face with his arms, upset the way he was. So just as I was leaving, I said, "Well, if they *do* ship me a thousand miles away from here, I might manage to hitch a ride back every once in a while," but it didnt do no good. He only moaned, his face still covered up and didnt answer me at all.

Chief White Halfoat

Joseph Heller

Chief White Halfoat was a handsome, swarthy Indian from Oklahoma with a heavy, hard-boned face and tousled black hair, a half-blooded Creek from Enid who, for occult reasons of his own, had made up his mind to die of pneumonia. He was a glowering, vengeful, disillusioned Indian who hated foreigners with names like Cathcart, Korn, Black and Havermeyer and wished they'd all go back to where their lousy ancestors had come from.

"You wouldn't believe it, Yossarian," he ruminated, raising his voice deliberately to bait Doc Daneeka, "but this used to be a pretty good country to live in before they loused it up with their goddam piety."

Chief White Halfoat was out to revenge himself upon the white man. He could barely read or write and had been assigned to Captain Black as assistant intelligence officer.

"How could I learn to read or write?" Chief White Halfoat demanded with simulated belligerence, raising his voice again so that Doc Daneeka would hear. "Every place we pitched our tent, they sank an oil well. Every time they sank a well, they hit oil. And every time they hit oil, they made us pack up our tent and go someplace else. We were human divining rods. Our whole family had a natural affinity for petroleum deposits, and soon every oil company in the world had technicians chasing us around. We were always on the move. It was one hell of a way to bring a child up, I can tell you. I don't think I ever spent more than a week in one place."

His earliest memory was of a geologist.

"Every time another White Halfoat was born," he continued, "the stock market turned bullish. Soon whole drilling crews were following us around with all their equipment just to get the jump on each other. Companies began to merge just so they could cut down on the number of people they had to assign to us. But the crowd in back of us kept growing. We never got a good night's sleep. When we stopped, they stopped. When we moved, they moved, chuckwagons, bulldozers, derricks, generators. We were a walking business boom, and we began to receive invitations from some of the best hotels just for the amount of business we would drag into town with us. Some of those invitations were mighty generous, but we couldn't accept any because we were Indians and all the best hotels that were inviting us wouldn't accept Indians as guests. Racial prejudice is a terrible thing, Yossarian. It really is. It's a terrible thing to treat a decent, loyal Indian like a nigger, kike, wop, or spic." Chief White Halfoat nodded slowly with conviction.

"Then, Yossarian, it finally happened—the beginning of the end. They began to follow us around from in front. They would try to guess where we were going to stop next and would begin drilling before we even got there, so we couldn't even stop. As soon as we'd begin to unroll our blankets, they would kick us off. They had confidence in us. They wouldn't even wait to strike oil before they kicked us off. We were so tired we almost didn't care the day our time ran out. One morning we found ourselves completely surrounded by oilmen waiting for us to come their way so they could kick us off. Everywhere you looked there was an oilman on a ridge, waiting there like Indians getting ready to attack. It was the end. We couldn't stay where we were because we had just been kicked off. And there was no place left for us to go. Only the Army saved me. Luckily, the war broke out just in the nick of time, and a draft board picked me right up out of the middle and put me down safely in Lowery Field, Colorado. I was the only survivor."

Yossarian knew he was lying, but did not interrupt as Chief White Halfoat went on to claim that he had never heard from his parents again. That didn't bother him too much, though, for he had only their word for it that they were his parents, and since they had lied to him about so many other things, they could just as well have been lying to him about that too. He was much better acquainted with the fate of a tribe of first cousins who had wandered away north in a diversionary movement and pushed inadvertently into Canada. When they tried to return, they were stopped at the border by American immigration authorities who would not let them back into the country. They could not come back in because they were red.

Dental or Mental, I Say It's Spinach

S. J. Perelman

A few days ago, under the heading, MAN LEAPS OUT
WINDOW AS DENTIST GETS FORCEPS, *The New York
Times* reported the unusual case of a man who leaped
out a window as the dentist got the forceps. Briefly,
the circumstances were these. A citizen in Staten Island tottered into a dental parlor and, indicating an
aching molar, moaned, "It's killing me. You've got to
pull it out." The dentist grinned like a Cheshire
cat—*The New York Times* neglected to say so, but a
Cheshire cat who was present at the time grinned like a
dentist—and reached for his instruments. "There was a
leap and crash," continues the account. "The astonished dentist saw his patient spring through the
closed window and drop ten feet to the sidewalk,
where he lay dazed." The casualty was subsequently
treated at a nearby hospital for abrasion and shock by
Drs. J. G. Abrazian and Walter Shock, and then, like
a worm, crept back to the dentist, apologized and
offered to pay for the damage. On one point, however,
he remained curiously adamant. He still has his tooth.

As a party who recently spent a whole morning with
his knees braced against a dentist's chest, whimpering
"Don't—don't—I'll do anything, but don't drill!" I
am probably the only man in America equipped to

sympathize with the poor devil. Ever since Nature presented me at birth with a set of thirty-two flawless little pearls of assorted sizes, I never once relaxed my vigilant stewardship of same. From the age of six onward, I constantly polished the enamel with peanut brittle, massaged the incisors twice daily with lollipops, and chewed taffy and chocolate-covered caramels faithfully to exercise the gums. As for consulting a dentist regularly, my punctuality practically amounted to a fetish. Every twelve years I would drop whatever I was doing and allow wild Caucasian ponies to drag me to a reputable orthodontist. I guess you might say I was hipped on the subject of dental care.

When, therefore, I inadvertently stubbed a tooth on a submerged cherry in an old-fashioned last week and my toupee ricocheted off the ceiling, I felt both dismayed and betrayed. By eleven the next morning, I was seated in the antechamber of one Russell Pipgrass, D.D.S., limply holding a copy of the *National Geographic* upside down and pretending to be absorbed in Magyar folkways. Through the door communicating with the arena throbbed a thin, bloodcurdling whine like a circular saw biting into a green plank. Suddenly an ear-splitting shriek rose above it, receding into a choked gurgle. I nonchalantly tapped out my cigarette in my eardrum and leaned over to the nurse; a Medusa type with serpents writhing out from under her prim white coif.

"Ah—er—pardon me," I observed, swallowing a bit of emery paper I had been chewing. "Did you hear anything just then?"

"Why, no," she replied, primly tucking back a snake under her cap. "What do you mean?"

"A—kind of a scratchy sound," I faltered.

"Oh, that," she sniffed carelessly. "Impacted wisdom tooth. We have to go in through the skull for those, you know." Murmuring some inconsequential excuse about lunching with a man in Sandusky, Ohio, I dropped to the floor and was creeping toward the corridor on all fours when Dr. Pipgrass emerged, rubbing his hands. "Well, here's an unexpected windfall!" he cackled, his eyes gleaming with cupidity. "Look out—slam the door on him!" Before I could dodge past, he pinioned me in a hammer lock and bore me, kicking and struggling, into his web. He was trying to wrestle me into the chair when the nurse raced in brandishing a heavy glass ash tray.

"Here, hit him with this!" she panted.

"No, no, we mustn't bruise him," muttered Pipgrass. "Their relatives always ask a lot of silly questions." They finally made me comfy by strapping me into the chair with a half a dozen towels, tilted my feet up and pried open my teeth with a spoon. "Now then, where are his X-rays?" demanded the doctor.

"We haven't any," returned the nurse. "This is the first time he's been here."

"Well, bring me any X-rays," her employer barked. "What difference does it make? When you've seen one tooth, you've seen them all." He held up the X-rays against the light and examined them critically. "Well, friend, you're in a peck of trouble," he said at length. "You may as well know the worst. These are the teeth of an eighty-year-old man. You got here just in time." Plucking a horrendous nozzle from the rack, he shot compressed air down my gullet that sent me into a strangled paroxysm, and peered curiously at my inlays.

"Who put those in, a steamfitter?" he sneered. "You ought to be arrested for walking around with a job like that." He turned abruptly at the rustle of greenbacks and glared at his nurse. "See here, Miss Smedley, how many times have I told you not to count the patient's money in front of him? Take the wallet outside and go through it there." She nodded shamefacedly and slunk out. "That's the kind of thing that creates a bad impression on the layman," growled Dr. Pipgrass, poking at my tongue with a sharp stick. "Now what seems to be the trouble in there?"

"Ong ong ong," I wheezed.

"H'm'm'm, a cleft palate," he mused. "Just as I feared. And you've got between four and five thousand cavities. While we're at it, I think we'd better tear out those lowers with a jackhammer and put in some nice expensive crowns. Excuse me." He quickly dialed a telephone number. "Is that you Irene?" he asked. "Russell. Listen, on that white mink coat we were talking about at breakfast—go right ahead, I've changed my mind. . . . No, I'll tell you later. He's filthy with it."

"Look, Doctor," I said with a casual yawn. "It's nothing really—just a funny tickling sensation in that rear tooth. I'll be back Tuesday—a year from Tuesday."

"Yes, yes," he interrupted, patting me reassuringly. "Don't be afraid now; this won't hurt a bit." With a slow, cunning smile, he produced from behind his back a hypodermic of the type used on brewery horses and, distending my lip, plunged it into the gum. The tip of my nose instantly froze, and my tongue took on the proportions of a bolt of flannel. I tried to cry out, but my larynx was out to lunch. Seizing the opportunity, Pipgrass snatched up his drill, took a firm purchase on my hair and teed off. A mixture of sensation roughly comparable to being alternately stilettoed and inflated with a bicycle pump overcame me; two thin wisps of smoke curled upward slowly from my ears. Fortunately, I had been schooled from boyhood to withstand pain without flinching, and beyond an occasional scream that rattled the windows, I bore myself with the stoicism of a red man. Scarcely ninety minutes later, Dr. Pipgrass thrust aside the drill, wiped his streaming forehead and shook the mass of protoplasm before him.

"Well, we're in the home stretch," he announced brightly, extracting a rubber sheet from a drawer. "We'll put this dam on you and fill her in a jiffy. You don't get claustrophobia, do you?"

"Wh-what's that?" I squeaked.

"Fear of being buried alive," he explained smoothly. "Kind of a stifling feeling. Your heart starts racing and you think you're going crazy. Pure imagination, of course." He pinned the rubber sheet over my face, slipped it over the tooth and left me alone with my thoughts. In less time than it takes to relate, I was a graduate member, *summa cum laude*, of the Claustrophobia Club. My face had turned a stunning shade of green, my heart was going like Big Ben, and a set of castanets in my knees was playing the "Malagueña." Summoning my last reserves of strength, I cast off my bonds and catapulted through the anteroom to freedom. I bequeathed Pipgrass a fleece-lined overcoat worth sixty-eight dollars, and he's welcome to it; I'll string along nicely with this big wad of chewing gum over my tooth. On me it looks good.

Comic Definitions

Ant—A small hard working insect that always finds time to go to picnics

Beet—A potato with high blood pressure

Climax—An axe used by mountain climbers

Deliver—A vital part of the body

Farmer—An outstanding man in his field

Gossip—Letting the chat out of the bag

Hotel—A place where you pay dollars for quarters

Information—How Air Force planes fly

Laplander—A clumsy person in a bus

Nursery—A bawl park

Out of bounds—A tired kangeroo

Pretzel—A double-jointed doughnut

Raisin—A worried grape

Tennis racket—A bunch of holes strung together

Zebra—A pony with venetian blinds

8.

1960-1969

American Humor Protests

Cartoon—John Gallagher
From the Back of the Bus—Dick Gregory
Introducing Tobacco to Civilization—Bob Newhart
Bunky—Jack Douglas
Absurd Riddles

Introduction

This was a period of prosperity and enormous growth in education, in which the country saw the development of the hippie and flower-child movement and also a tremendous drive for full equality on the part of blacks and women. "Doing your own thing" was winning acceptance as a philosophy, while large institutions such as the Pentagon, the government bureaucracy, or General Motors came under attack by an increasingly vocal minority. The distant war in Viet Nam, at first barely noticed but supported generally, became unpopular and divisive.

Comedy now branched into new directions, much of it satirical and derisive. Black comics such as Dick Gregory, biting in his comment on the old values and old traditions now becoming shopworn, emerged. *MAD*, the *National Lampoon* and other parody magazines attacked the rich, the powerful, the entrenched.

Individual freedom and human rights, honesty, common sense, and democratic openness were still the values the country held dear. But the old love of nonsense as expressed by comedians Bob Newhart, Jonathan Winters, and Sid Caesar had an edge of irony added to it now. Woody Allen, in a reiteration of Chaplin's view of the world, devoted his humor—as reflected in stories, movies, plays—to a wry picture descriptive of the helplessness of the individual confronted by a computer-operated world, perhaps gone slightly mad.

1

2

3

4

From the Back of the Bus

Dick Gregory
A Black View

It's kinda hard to describe how we feel about Cadillacs. It's like riding around town in your own bank account. . . . 300 horsepower calling out to the world: "Hello, dere!" . . . GMAC's gift to gracious living. . . . I like it! I like it! . . .

Kids lead a tough life. Nobody takes them seriously. Nobody listens to them. They're always getting pushed aside. Kids and my people have a lot in common. . . . Only our problems aren't solved by getting older. . . . If man could only get a little older a little later, and a little wiser a little younger.

I had an uncle who was a practicing nudist down in Georgia—only no one knew it. Up North, you go around with a few rags on your back and you're called a sun worshipper. In Georgia, you're called a tenant farmer. . . . But he had some interesting ideas on nudism. He felt if everyone took off their clothes, there'd be no war—cause you couldn't tell your own soldiers from the enemy. And everybody agreed he had a good idea—right up to the Congo. . . . I'll tell you one thing about having naked soldiers. It'd sure make for some wild parades on Decoration Day! . . .

People keep askin' me why they don't send white troops to the Congo. They should be able to figure it out for themselves—war brides!

I have a lot of fun in the summer time. People come up, slap me on the back and I say: "Watch it! My sunburn!"—And you'd be surprised how many apologies I get! . . .

Baseball is very big with my people. It figures. It's the only time we can get to shake a bat at a white man without starting a riot.

You gotta say this for the white race—its self-confidence knows no bounds. Who else could go to a small island in the South Pacific where there's no poverty, no crime, no unemployment, no war and no worry—and call it a "primitive society"?

Introducing Tobacco to Civilization

Bob Newhart
Recording Routine

Milestones are not really recognized right away, it takes, oh, 50 or 60 years before people realize what an achievement it is. Like take for instance, tobacco and the discovery of tobacco.

It was discovered by Sir Walter Raleigh and he sent it over to England from the colonies. It seems that the uses of tobacco aren't obvious right off the bat. I imagine a phone conversation between Sir Walter Raleigh and the head of the West Indies Company in England, explaining about the shipment of tobacco that he just sent over. I think it would go something like this:

Yeh, who is it, Mary?

It's Sir Walter Raleigh from the colony.

Yeh, put him on.

Harry, you want to pick up the extension. It's nutty Walt again. Hi, Walt baby, how are you guy, how is everything going? Things are fine here, Walt.

Did we get the what? The boat load of turkeys? They arrived fine, Walt. As a matter of fact they're still here, Walt, they're wandering all over London, as a matter of fact.

See that's an American holiday, Walt.

What is it this time Walt, you got another winner for us do you? Tobacco? What's tobacco? Walt. It's a kind of a leaf and you bought 80 tons of it. Let me get this straight, now Walt, you bought 80 tons of leaves? This may come as kind of a surprise Walt, but come fall in England we are up to our . . .

It isn't that kind of a leaf. What is it a special food of some kind is it, Walt?

Not exactly, it has a lot of different uses. Like what are some of the uses, Walt? Are you saying snuff? What's snuff? You take a pinch of tobacco and shove it up your nose and it makes you sneeze. I imagine it would, Walt. Gee, a goldenrod seems to do it pretty well with us, Walt.

It has some other uses though. You can chew it, or put it on a piece of paper and roll it out. . . Don't tell me, Walt, don't tell me. You stick it in your ear, right, Walt? Walt, I hope you clean your lips. Then what do you do to it.

You set fire to it, Walt? Then what do you do? You inhale the smoke. You know, Walt, it seems off hand you can stand in front of your fireplace and have the same thing going for you, Walt. You see, Walt, we've been a little worried about you, you know, ever since you put your cape down over that mud.

You know, Walt, I think you're going to have a tough time telling people to stick burning leaves in their mouths.

It's going very big over there is it? What's the matter, Walt? You spilled your what? Your coffee? What's coffee, Walt? That's a drink you make out of beans, uh? That's going over very big there too is it?

A lot of people have their coffee after their first

cigarette in the morning. Is that what you call burning leaves, Walt, cigarettes?

I'll tell you what, Walt, why don't you send us a boat load of those beans too, if you can talk people into putting those burning leaves in their mouths, they gotta go for those beans.

Listen, Walt, don't call us, we'll call you.

Bunky

Jack Douglas

Bunky is a kid who lives in the neighborhood. This is a supposition. He may not be a kid who lives in the neighborhood. He may just be a leprechaun who lives in a hollow tree with the old hooty owl. And how he gets in the house, we'll never know. We look around, and he's there, solemnly staring at us, his light blue eyes, with their stationary lids, never changing expression. The first time Bunky surprised us his first words were: "If you want to talk to an eagle—just get an eagle."

"Who are you?" I said.

"I'm Bunky."

"Where do you live?"

"Over there," he said, pointing at everywhere.

I said, "Oh." Then, "This is Bobby." And Bobby immediately ran to his mother. The way Bunky looked at us, I wanted to do the same thing. Then, in order to make him feel at home and perhaps get Bobby to release his grip on Reiko, I said brilliantly, "What do you wanna be when you grow up?"

He said, "A bloodsucker."

I said, "You wanna watch television?"

He said, "Don't you wanna know why I wanna be a bloodsucker when I grow up?"

Bobby said, "*I* do."

Then Reiko said, "Bobby, you'll have bad dreams tonight."

I said, "What about me?"

And she said, "We're going to have spaghetti and meatballs for dinner."

Then Bobby said to Reiko, "Mommie, you know what I wanna be when I grow up—a bloodsucker."

Reiko said, "Wouldn't you rather have spaghetti and meatballs?"

"I would," said Bunky.

I said, "Okay—but we'd better call your mother and tell her you're eating with us. Do you know your telephone number?"

He said, "No, but we're on Channel Nine."

I said, "What's your last name? I'll look your phone number up in the book."

Bunky said, "I'm a guest."

I said, "Yes, that's right, but—"

He continued, "Guests can do anything they want except make loud noise."

Bobby is something like Bunky, except that we know who his parents are. One day after his fifth Christmas when Santa had brought him a real wristwatch that really ticked and the hands moved and everything, I became slightly annoyed with him because, although I get up at 5:00 A.M. in order to work, he gets up about fifteen minutes later in order to get in a full day of play, which he starts by using the top of my desk as a base for his vast fleet of jet airplanes. The sonic boom, furnished by Bobby is almost unbearable when I'm trying to write a tender story of the love of a humpbacked midget and a spastic flower child (for Off-Broadway).

On this particular day I became so irritated, I said, "You know what I'm going to do, Bobby—I'm going to exchange you for a girl!"

He stopped a 727 jet takeoff in midair and sneered, "She won't have a wristwatch!"

Before I answered *this*, I tried to remember from Dr. Haim Ginott's book *Between Parent and Child* (New Solutions to Old Problems) just what I should say. I remembered some of the things you shouldn't say, to quote Dr. Ginott, like: "You are a disgrace to your school and no credit to your family!" or "You will end up in a federal penitentiary, that's where you'll end up!" or "If you don't settle down and stop flying those goddamn airplanes in front of my face while I'm sitting at my desk working you can forget about your allowance for this week—and next week, too!" Those are the things one shouldn't say, and I'm sorry, because they seem so appropriate and comforting. To me.

On another icy morning in late January, I was hunched over my old old old Remington portable (it's so old the *s*'s come out *f*'s). I thought this was to be my lucky morning because Bobby had not shown up. I was working in peace and relative quiet, except for the howling wind, which seemed to be testing our picture windows' tensile strength. This placid situation was not to last. No sooner had I lost myself in the writer's enforced dream world when Bobby thumped into my life with his size 18 sneakers. He was tearing the clothes off an almost life-sized Captain Marvel plastic doll.

"What the hell are you doing?!!!" I screamed, in my best Father-of-the-Year voice.

"Shut up!" he said.

Slipping my machete out of my belt, I said, "You are a disgrace to your school and no credit to your family!"

"Shut up," he said.

I said, "Look you little—devil—one more 'shut up' and I'll cut your heart out!"

Then he looked up at me with his big brown eyes and said, "Papa, I'm glad you don't go to New York to work every day. I like it when you stay home all the time."

I said, "Okay. Okay. Now what in the hell are you doing to Captain Marvel? Why did you rip all of his clothes off?"

"I'm gonna play Jesus and Captain Marvel is gonna be Jesus."

"I thought you liked Captain Marvel the way he was."

"I do," he said, "but Jesus is better than Captain Marvel. That's what Bunky said."

"Oh," I said. "Where does Bunky get all of this inside information?"

"*Time* magazine."

"What?"

"That's what Bunky said."

Most of the children in our neighborhood seem well behaved enough except for Charlie and Madge's seven-and nine-year-olds, Durward and Googie. They look like two angels from heaven, with their long blond curls and their baby blue innocent eyes, but they are terrors. They have set their own house on fire countless

times and have been, I heard, the reason for the Old
New Litchridge Volunteer Fire Department losing too
many members to other hobbies.

Durward and Googie's arsonist activities seem to be
limited to their own home—on the outside their specialty is empty houses, or houses under construction.
They are drawn like unwary sailors to the Lorelei of
unbroken windows. This, Durward and Googie feel, is
an intolerable condition. Windows were made to be
broken. And broken they are. Such is their fascination
with this type of destruction, I'm sure it will become a
fetish, and in later years when they hop into bed with
some willing female, they'll take a quick glance around
for an unbroken window, and their lovemaking may be
slightly handicapped by a rock in each hand—ready for
the climactic moment.

Durward and Googie are picked up regularly by the
cops and always admit readily that they have broken
windows, stolen bicycles, canoes or fishing poles, or
have exploded firecrackers in Old Lady Penrose's gar-
bage can just as she was bending over to flick an aphid
off her lilies of the valley. There is nothing that can be
done with this pair until they are sixteen, and most of
Old New Litchridge's police officers are marking off
the days on the walls of their locker room—like the
Count of Monte Cristo.

Bobby and *every* kid in town are at their worst at the
A & P. There is just too much to grab, and they take
full advantage. There isn't a mother who hasn't arrived
at the check-out counter not to be made aghast at the
armful of goodies her dear little one has snatched on
the way. Crackerjacks, Baby Ruths, plastic bags full of
lollipops, miniature cars, tiny airplanes, midget pre-

historic monsters, assorted dolls, nonassorted dolls, jelly beans, plastic pinwheels, gumballs, silly putty, sober putty, half-eaten boxes of Animal Crackers, and, sometimes for the more erudite, a movie magazine or two.

The mother at this time has two choices: Let the child *keep* its purloined prizes, *return* everything to its proper section, or *shoot* the child right between the eyes and claim temporary sanity. Better make that *three* choices.

Most mothers start their children on the road to juvenile delinquency right at the A & P. They let the little darlings keep the loot and gladly (more or less) pay for it. Bobby has yet to come from there without some little trinket to show him we love him.

Bunky came home from the A & P one day with a fifteen-pound smoked ham. We found this out from him long after. When I asked him why he wanted a fifteen-pound smoked ham, he said because he had nobody to play with. He calls it Shirley. There may be more to Bunky than meets the eye. I have a feeling that someday Bunky will become even more successful than the Boston Strangler. With branch offices in Lexington, Concord, Zanesville, Ohio, and Paris, France.

Bunky isn't the only genius in our neighborhood. Bobby has shown some signs of above-average imagination. I have a small Saudi Arabian flag hanging in my office, a souvenir of a visit to Abdul's East, a tiny East Side (NYC) restaurant whose specialty was chocolate-covered sheep eyes, which are considered to be a great delicacy anywhere east of Baghdad. This Saudi Arabian flag has always fascinated Bobby because of the Arabic lettering and the large curved Oriental sword on it. One day, he could contain himself no longer. "Papa," he said, "what kind of flag is that —American?" I said, "No—guess again." He said, "Stamford?" I didn't have the heart to say no. Also, I couldn't be so sure.

Bobby, like all children, uses our language to suit his purpose, an art which we lose forever after we have learned, or have been told thousands of times, the limitations inside of which we are supposed to stay. He, almost since he first learned to talk, has called me "Papa-boy." After a while he called Reiko "Mamma-boy." And during the summer the playmates he finds while digging in the dirt are called "Worm-boy."

But children are very nice to have if you want to know something about your neighbors. All you have to do is invite *their* children over to play with *yours*, and what they don't volunteer you can find out by a few chosen queries like, "Does your father go to work in New York every day?" "What kind of car do you have?" "Do you have many parties at your house?" "Do you have a mortgage?" Very few are able to answer this last, but most kids being stool pigeons at heart, with their morning milk well laced with truth serum, they just love to spill their guts. Actually this kind of thing is dirty pool, and as much as I'd like to know what the hell does go with some of our more exotic near-friends, I abstain—except on rare occasions when on the day somebody new moves into the neighborhood, and I casually notice (through my 70-power binoculars) the arrival of a tall dark man wearing long white flowing robes and very black sunglasses followed by thirty-five or forty veiled women riding camels. I don't have to be told that here is a guy who has it *made*. Either that or we're in for a long, hard winter of costume parties.

Absurd Riddles

What do you get when you cross a cat with a lemon?
A sour puss

What's gray and has a trunk?
A mouse going on vacation.

What's purple and swims?
Moby grape.

What's yellow and weighs 1,000 pounds?
Two 500 pound canaries.

What is the best way to catch a rabbit?
Hide behind a bush and make a sound like a carrot.

What do you get when you cross a movie with a
swimming pool?
A dive-in theatre.

What goes tick, tick, choo, tick, tick, choo?
A clock with a cold.

What's white outside, green inside and hops?
A frog sandwich.

Bibliography

Suggestions for Further Reading

Becker, Stephen. Comic Art in America, Simon and Schuster, 1959.

Blair, Walter, ed. Native American Humor, 1960.

Cerf, Bennett, ed. Encyclopedia of Modern American Humor. Doubleday, 1954.

Curtis, Richard. The Genial Idiots. Crowell, Collier, 1968.

Geng, Veronica, ed. In a Fit of Laughter, Platt and Munk, 1969.

Hughes, Langston, ed. The Book of Negro Humor, Dodd, Mead, 1967.

Littell, Joseph F., Ed. The Comic Spirit. Lothrop, Lee and Shepard, 1975.

Rourke, Constance. American Humor. Harcourt, Brace, 1931.

Stillman, Deanne and Beatts, Anne, eds. Titters. Collier, 1976.

Tidwell, James N., Ed. A Treasury of American Folk Humor, Crown, 1950.

Untermeyer, Louis, ed. Treasury of Great Humor, McGraw Hill, 1972.

Weber, Brom, ed. An Anthology of American humor, Crowell, 1962.

White, E. B. and Katherine S., eds. A Subtreasury of American Humor, Capricorn, 1962.

Index

Abbott and Costello, 188
Abe Lincoln's Jokes, 51
Absurd Riddles, 292
Alibi Ike, 134
Alden, W. L. 75
Another Uncle Edith Christmas Story, 163

Benchley, Robert, 163
Big Bear of Arkansas, The, 52
Branner, Martin, 132, 133
Briggs, Clare, 66, 67
Bunky, 285
Bunner, H. C., 79
Burns and Allen, 256

Cartoons, 61, 62, 64-67, 131, 162, 202, 236
Charles, 222
Chief White Halfoat, 264
Clemens, Samuel L. (See Mark Twain), 68
Comic Definitions, 273
Comic Strips, 63, 132, 133
Coon-Skin Trick, The, 36

Crockett, Davy, 36
Danforth, Samuel, 5
Day, Clarence, 174
Dental or Mental, I Say It's Spinach, 267
Dirks, Rudolph, 63
Douglas, Jack, 285
Dr. Kronkhite, 143

Early American Gravestones, 123
Epitaph On a Patient Killed by a Cancer Quack, 12
Epitaph Written, 1728, 9

Father Opens My Mail, 174
Fibber McGee and Molly, 203
Flies, The, 10
Franklin, Benjamin, 9, 10
From the Back of the Bus, 280

Gallagher, John, 278, 279
Gibson, Charles Dana, 64

Glorious Whitewasher, The, 68

Gracie Talks About Her Relatives, 256

Gregory, Dick, 280

Heller, Joseph, 264

Henry, O., 99

Heroic People of Windham, The, 27

His Pa Plays Jokes, 94

Hopkins, Lemuel, 12

Howarth, F. M., 61

Hyman, Mac, 259

Introducing Tobacco to Civilization, 282

Irving, Washington, 29

Jackson, Shirley, 222

Jane, 113

Katzenjammer Kids, 63

Kelly, Eldon, 131

Knock, Knock Jokes, 157

Lardner, Ring, 134

Lincoln, Abraham, 51

Little Moron Jokes, 229

Marx Brothers, 151

Mauldin, Bill, 202

Mayer, Hy, 62

Miller, Joe, Jokes, 18

Newhart, Bob, 282

Night the Bed Fell, The, 168

No Time for Sergeants, 259

Patented Child, A, 75

Peck, George, 94

Pencil-Chewing, 183

Perelman, S. J., 267

Peters, Samuel A., 27

Porges, Paul Peter, 236

Radio Show, 203

Ransom of Red Chief, The, 99

Robinson, Boardman, 65

She Shall Have Music, 237

She Was Only Jokes, 196

Shulman, Max, 237

Smith and Dale, 143

Song, A Patriotic, 15

Sullivan, Frank, 183

Tarkington, Booth, 113

Television Show, 256

Thorpe, T. B., 42

Thurber, James, 168

Twain, Mark, 68

Untermeyer, Louis, 211

Verses for Every Month in the Year, 5

Who's on First?, 188
Why a Duck?, 151
Williams, J. R., 162
Winnie Winkle, 132, 133

Wonderful Adventures of Paul Bunyan, The, 211
Wouter Van Twiller, 29

Yankee Doodle, 15
Yankee Exaggerations, 54

Zenobia's Infidelity, 79

817.008
Lau

1219 80
8.95

AUTHOR

TITLE
Laughing

DATE DUE	BORROWER'S NAME
FEB 2 4 198	Black +2
⑫	ns 3/3 3/31 4/2
APR 2 198	Diana Trujillo FA2 Ponstler 10
DEC 13 1982	Sr. 12
NO 29 84	

817.008
Lau

1219 80
8.95

Laughing

SANTA FE HIGH SCHOOL
LIBRARY